Post War Boy

Volume Two: Starting Out in Newfoundland, Mexico, London, Milton Keynes and Derbyshire...

Iain ~ thanks for your help
with the Newfie chapter.

Some stun,

Trevor

About the Author

Trevor Cherrett is a semi-retired rural community planner, a member of the Town & Country Planning Association policy council and Chair of the Wiltshire Community Land Trust. He has written a first volume memoir of *Post War Boy*, growing up as a post war baby boomer on the south coast; and *Slow Boats to Europe*, the story of a river journey from the English Channel to the Black Sea. He is also a regular contributor to boating and fishing magazines.

Post War Boy

Volume Two: Starting Out in Newfoundland, Mexico, London, Milton Keynes and Derbyshire...

Trevor Cherrett

Matador
9 Priory Business Park,
Wistow Road, Kibworth Beauchamp,
Leicestershire, LE8 0RX
Tel: 0116 279 2299
Email: books@troubador.co.uk
Web: www.troubador.co.uk/matador
Twitter: @matadorbooks

ISBN 978 1789018 271

British Library Cataloguing in Publication Data.
A catalogue record for this book is available from the British Library.

Printed and bound by CPI Group (UK) Ltd, Croydon, CR0 4YY
Typeset in 11pt Aldine401 BT by Troubador Publishing Ltd, Leicester, UK

Matador is an imprint of Troubador Publishing Ltd

To baby boomers everywhere, and their descendants

Contents

Preface

Starting Out is the second volume of my memoirs as a baby boomer, tracing my life after graduation through jobs, travel and marriage.

It simply sets out how things seemed to me during the 1970s: working abroad, returning to London, getting married, and moving north to Derbyshire. Like Volume One it is also concerned with the *places* that I lived and worked and played in, with a particular professional perspective on how those environments were planned and governed.

Starting Out is a personal recollection, inevitably partial, and coloured by my personal and emotional experiences. Inevitably, it involves other people. I hope that any observations I have made have been reasonable and fair: I intended that any judgements I may have made, whether explicit or implicit, have been directed more at myself than others. And some names have been changed or omitted to avoid embarrassments. In the end of course any distortions, and indeed omissions, are my responsibility. As such it`s aims are modest: a subjective testament from one life led during this pivotal decade of economic decline, cultural turbulence and political change.

Trevor Cherrett
November 2018

Chapter 1

Newfoundland & Labrador

I am gazing down at a moonscape of bare rocks, lightened by ponds and scrubby forests. There is hardly a building, let alone a person, to be seen. This is New Found Land, as John Cabot described it from his pioneering passage in the *Matthew* in 1497. Only a few hours ago I was saying my goodbyes at Heathrow, now I feel as if I'm on another planet – as Cabot might have done, given that he only stayed 3 weeks.

My plane lands at Gander, the international airport built for the post-war propeller planes that had to stop for re-fuelling. The only other planes on the runway apron are a tired looking Cuban Airways *Illyushin* transporter – a refugee from the US embargo – and a few light aircraft. The Arrivals Lounge is vast, modern and empty. Its windows gaze out onto a bleak, empty landscape. I am beginning to wonder if this emigration, to my first proper job, was a good idea.

"Yawannewurks? "asks the aproned young man behind the counter. "Er, yes I suppose so" I reply diffidently. The "works" comprise mustard, green relish, catsup (ketchup) and 1000 Island Dressing on my cheeseburger. I am surprised how scrumptious it is – I never tasted anything like this in England.

I change flights to an Eastern Provincial Airways [EPA] *DC – 4 Corvair* to St John's, the capital of the Province. The land below stays rocky, wooded, uninhabited. What have I come to – will there be proper shops, music, civilisation? I am losing perspective.

But I have met up with a fellow emigrant, Jim, one of six new recruits to the Provincial Planning Office. He is from Northern Ireland, a little older than me, reserved, with a mature and darkly humorous intelligence. I feel some relief – there is at least one other sane person at this place.

We are booked in at the Holiday Inn at St John's, which for all its size (over 100,000 population) still feels pretty raw, remote. Telegraph poles and wires festoon wide tarmacked roads and concrete buildings spaced out over rock and scrub. The office has kindly arranged for us to be met at the Holiday Inn by a senior officer from the Government of Newfoundland & Labrador's Department of Planning & Municipal Affairs – my new employers. It is 1968, and this is my first job.

"Hello chaps, had a good flight?"

Jim and I murmer assent.

"Well, here you are, well done. Smashing hotel to stay at, and we can put you on to some nice accommodation near the lake. Bit expensive, but all mod cons. And everybody is really friendly – you'll have a great time. "

We chat, and he is jolly, extrovert and friendly, like the secretary of the Social Club, or perhaps a Union rep. But gradually I realise he is our boss, a deputy head of the Department. I am fresh out from Manchester University, full of know-all ambition, and wondering if I have come a bit too far into the boondocks.

But he is helpful. As advised, we rent rooms in *Lakeview Apartments*, a new block of flats overlooking a lake called *Quid Vidi Pond*: each apartment is a reasonably sized bedsitter, with an adjoining kitchen and loo. Quite expensive, so we share it, probably at my insistence. After all, it was an improvement on sharing a bedroom with two other students ...

St John's is a city of two worlds. The old port, with tired but elegant clapboard terraces running steeply down to the quay and its streets of shops and stores; then the new sprawling loops of roads, shopping malls and housing estates. We have no car so we walk to the shops, humping large brown bags back to our apartment. Nobody else does this. Jim has lived in Canada before but I am experiencing a culture shock at a place where an old colonial culture has been all but replaced by a modern American society, even if a couple of years behind the times (the "Newfie Lag"). And the locals are very friendly, uninhibitedly curious and helpful, with a distinctive if often unintelligible Irish/Canadian accent. "My oh my, some stun" translates roughly as "that's amazing". And, starting a first job in a totally foreign country, I am emotionally, intellectually, and culturally "some stun".

3

*St John`s: a 19th century city with 20th century transport,
running down to the harbour*

* * *

Jim and I settle in to our apartment. He has a dignity
and propriety quite absent from the culture which I had
absorbed at university – the loose, mildly rebellious,
let-it-all-hang-out attitudes of the baby boomers in
England. I am taken aback by his freshly polished shoes
and his careful, judicious observations. Jim comes from
an Ulster Presbyterian background, although no longer
holding any religious beliefs; he carries an upright
approach to life which I recognise faintly from my
own Protestant background. He must be feeling a little
aggrieved to be sharing accommodation and job title with
someone straight out of college like me, who appears to

have all the answers without any of the experience to justify them.

Work involves a commute to Confederation Building, a huge municipal style building on a hill at the edge of the city. We have joined 'Joey's boys', civil servants of the Province of Newfoundland & Labrador, whose Premier is Joey Smallwood, a populist veteran from the post-war settlement in which the province decided by referendum to throw in its lot with Canada. The other options were to go independent or – a wild card – join the United States of America. The choice made was essentially one of security – the Canadian Federal Government would financially support the ailing eastern seaboard province. In the post-war boom years that is exactly what happened: the' Feds' effectively bankrolled a province whose fisheries were failing, and which could not find alternative viable economic activity beyond the iron ore of the Labrador mines, the timber from the west coast, and a succession of frontier resource rushes mostly fronted by dubious American adventurers seeking a quick buck. Meanwhile a substantial proportion of the population was surviving on welfare handouts provided by Ottawa. Some argued that this dependency on the federal nation had undermined the old independent spirit and resilience of 'newfies', and that the province was being killed by kindness. But it was too late now.

By the time we arrived there were already rumbling accusations of corruption at the highest level, linked to the interests of freebooting entrepreneurs, and a growing sense that Joey's long post war reign was outliving its stay in the changing times of the late 1960s. But for the moment the old regime was still in power. Confederation Building was populated by floors of professional and technical officers, cohorts of administrators and clerks, and platoons of politicians, mostly low profile junior Ministers. 'Joey' was the undisputed political leader, not averse to intervening in technical matters such as a minor planning dispute – the sort of political intervention which was highly 'irregular' to British administrators then (but perhaps less so now). His presence dominated almost everything the Province engaged in.

But as professionals in a new planning department carved out by 'Colonel'[1] Jack Allston, the avuncular but shrewd Director who had interviewed me in London, we had a relatively free rein to carry out planning based on the UK legislative set-up. The Colonel had two senior deputies – one of whom was our one-man welcome committee – who covered the legislation and much of the day-to-day political firefighting and who managed two teams of two to three development planners who undertook 'municipal plans' (similar to UK Local Plans) throughout the province. The territory was carved up: mine alone covered two peninsulas on the mainland, and the whole of Labrador! We also took on province-wide studies connected with leisure, lakeside recreational cabins, and proposed national parks. In terms of land area it was like planning the whole of the UK, but with a population of only 400,000.

So work consisted of a conventional nine-to-five day in the offices of Confederation Building, complete with

---

1   Mr Allston was always embarrassed by the 'Colonel' title, which he gained in the Territorials. But the nomenclature suited him, and it stuck.

tea breaks and lunch in the CNIB (Canadian National Institute for the Blind) canteen, interspersed with EPA flights to far flung parts of the island and Labrador, and/ or long car rides across the TransCanada Highway – in my case in a hired Plymouth Fury Mk 3 playing Arthur Brown's "I Am The God of Hellfire" at full volume. A site visit might involve a two – hour flight, a five – hour drive and an overnight stay in a snowbound motel. I loved it.

But there was a certain dissonance between my college – learnt techniques and processes for planning town and country in a relatively sophisticated nation and dealing with the basic problems of communities which had grown up around fishing, timber management, and mineral extraction. These communities ranged from the old 'outports', little fishing settlements of clapboard houses and fish – drying platforms ('flakes') strung along the shore, to larger and more modern towns built to serve large scale resource exploitation, such as Corner Brook for the timber business (pulp for newspaper) in western Newfoundland, and Labrador City for extracting iron ore. Others were specifically linked to American and British defence bases: Stephenville in western Newfoundland, Goose Bay in Labrador. The immediate problems facing these settlements were more concerned with basic infrastructure – water, sewerage, electricity etc, and the fundamental economic and social problems arising from such great dependence on single activities, rather than the nuanced technicalities of growth patterns and journey-to-work movements characteristic of contemporary 'structure planning' in the UK.

I did my best, not without *some* imagination. My proposed 'skidoo ways' went down well in Happy Valley, a predominantly Inuit[2] community attached to the USAF Base at Goose Bay, only to be revoked by a change of local administration at a subsequent election. The burnt orange shades of my local plan map caused as much amusement in my St John's office as in Labrador. But I was excited to be making my first proper (statutory) Plan, wholly conceived and managed by myself, at a time in my career when most of my contemporaries in England would have still been in very junior support roles.

★ ★ ★

"Come on Mr Shirt, we're off to Bonne Bay".

It's my team leader, John Bosworth. "Shirt" was my new nickname, a Newfie corruption of Cherrett. Someone in the office had also mistakenly called me "Don", so my new name was Don Shirt. New job, new name …

John was a charismatic design planner with great imagination and a predilection for offbeat, sometimes wild humour. "We've got a fortnight to plan a new *national park*", he tells me.

Bonne Bay, later called *Gros Morne*, comprises a cordillera of very high hills forming the backdrop to a beautiful coastline of bays, fiords, and fishing communities along the west coast of Newfoundland.

---

2   At that time we referred to the local population as *Eskimo*, with the term *Inuit* reserved for the small indigenous communities across Labrador

Our job is to delineate the boundary of the Park, taking on the contentious issue of whether the boundary should be drawn round the outside of existing communities to obviate the necessity of moving them if they were inside – a fundamental principle of Canadian (and US) National Parks. After a long discussion in the office, typically characterised by prim ideological theories on my part and gruff, practical wisdom on John's, we decide that we should move the boundaries rather than the communities.

Rather than take the plane, John decides that we will *drive* the 400 miles or so to the west coast in his little red *Mini*. Rex, the office technician, accompanies us. He has a big smile and an engaging sense of humour, which he will need.

We stay over at a small motel. It is bitterly cold, and John turns the heating up in the little room that we share. By 2am my brow is damp. By 3am I am sweating heavily. Suddenly Rex leaps out of bed.

"Jesus, me-boys, it's cod hot in here" he cries, opening the external door. A blast of snow whirls into the room.

"Whaaa" yells John. Rex slams the door back, while John struggles out and gropes around for the heating switch. We can't find the light and we are shifting around the room like ferrets in a sack. Eventually we sort out the heating and collapse back onto our beds. But it takes some time to get to sleep again.

Bonne Bay is beautiful. We have a great time touring the whole area, working out the boundary issues. It is a satisfying, practical job with a clear aim and result. Our report is well received. Many years later I revisited

*Bonne Bay: we planned to keep small coastal communities such as this
intact by drawing the proposed national park boundary outside them.*

the area to find that the Park has been created with
great sensitivity and skill, enhancing and highlighting
its landscape, waterscape, and geology. Boats take you
into the fiords, where very ancient rocks of geological
significance are exposed on the hillsides. Whether the
communities were thriving I was not able to tell, but
they looked in reasonable shape.[3]

★ ★ ★

"Here, me-boy, have a moose sandwich".

---

3   Years later I was fortunate enough to undertake a study of
     similar communities in New Zealand and Australia, courtesy of
     the excellent Winston Churchill Fellowship.

Pastor Reid, the leader of a small community on the west coast, is talking to us in a small hut, somewhere up in the forest above the shore. We – John, myself, Pastor Reid and a couple of his flock – are taking a break from searching for a fresh water supply for a site that he has selected to re-locate his whole community, by towing the houses along the coast by boat.

The moose filling has been forked out of a dubious looking jar on a shelf in the hut. Well, I think, there are no snakes in Newfie, maybe there's no botulism…; it tastes like tough stewing steak. No doubt it will get you through a cold, wet and windy day.

"Thanks very much" I say, holding the huge doorstep tentatively with both hands. John grins. He is on the case – sceptical about Pastor Reid and his magic water spring, and determined to check it out thoroughly. I haven't a clue. I might as well be Rupert Bear in some wild woodland adventure.

Moving whole communities was not an issue confined to national parks. Encouraging small, remote communities to up-sticks and move to larger ones – sometimes, like Pastor Reid was proposing, moving whole homes by boat along the shore – was the prevailing policy in the Province, administered by a separate Department, in order to concentrate the provision of healthcare, education and services of all kinds in one location. Clearly it was easier and cheaper to provide these services in a few larger settlements, and the Provincial Government offered incentives. Pastor Reid was keen to take advantage, and he had the whole community behind him.

But he wasn't typical. Many communities felt undermined, even bullied, by the Provincial Government, and many critics felt that this policy simply extended the disastrous trend of creating greater dependence on welfare. Small 'outports' might lack services, but people could get by with a mix of inshore fishing and growing a few vegetables, building their own homes rather than being drawn into large mortgages in a newly built home in a new centre. Whether these criticisms owed more to sentiment than reality or not, the policy was being seriously reviewed by the time we started our work as planners, to the extent that the re-location of settlements became strictly by consent only, and all notions of enforcement were removed. This would not however have removed the difficulty of making services available to existing small communities.

"Look, there's a *'hotter'*" cries Pastor Reid, as we lumber down to the shore. We gaze at the sea, looking for the sea otter known to frequent this coast. We can't see it. "It's in the same place as the spring" mutters John under his breath, "in his head". Our report is inconclusive.

* * *

Meanwhile in St John's a more conventional urban lifestyle prevailed – shopping in the old port or the new malls for example. Outside the city we – mostly the recently recruited gang of 'ex-pats' – drove out for trips round the Bay, or on Telegraph Hill where Marconi sent his first cables, and where Alcock and Brown had taken off for their historic first flight across the Atlantic. In the evening there were bars for drinking, notably the 'Tudor Inn' run by an anglophile landlord who had served in the RAF in the war. He encouraged live jazz and dancing – personally facilitated by sprinklings of talcum powder on the floor – and this became our (ex-pat) hang out on weekend evenings.

There were also parties. The arrival of some young professional Brits had not gone unnoticed and there were several social events often initiated by one of the senior planner's wives, who was a leading light in the city's theatre scene. It was at one of these parties that I met Maureen, a lively blonde who was as bright as she was sassy. We hit it off from the start. I felt like I was falling off the proverbial log …

But not right away. The following day I was heading off to the Northern Peninsula with some local planners. The Colonel had shrewdly suggested that I undertake this trip to get to know the country and its people. I flew to Corner Brook with one of the senior (Newfie) planners, where we met local officers who took us on up the Northern Peninsula by car. I sat in the back, and was having trouble understanding their Newfie accents, the exact nature of the mission, and getting Maureen (and too many beers) out of my head. Rupert Bear was lost again.

As we sped northwards it began to snow, and snow hard. After a couple of hours we were in a 'whiteout' and I could hardly see a thing. My two colleagues in the front did not seem too worried, and soon we came to a stop outside a white clapboard house, one of hundreds of white clapboard houses we had ghosted by in the snow. But this one must have been special – there was a warm welcome, and a hot broth containing all kinds of weird bits of meat and fish – the famous local *fish'n'brewis*. I still couldn't catch the local dialect properly. I felt that I was in some kind of incomprehensible dream journey, and the rest of the trip passed by in a blur. We eventually reached St Anthony at the northern tip, home of the historic Grenfell Mission. But all I wanted to do was get back to St John's and see Maureen....

When I got back I realised that my feelings for Maureen were not imaginary. I had easily and swiftly "fallen in love". She was great company and we fancied each other to bits. She loved my 'quaint' English accent and style, and I loved her direct, engaging manner. All of which at first obscured the many cultural differences between us, or the small matter of other relationships. But for the most part we were a natural 'item'.

"Come on Trevor, let's go out to the Old Colonial," she said one evening. Here we drank, ate steaks, and watched half-baked 'burlesque' which passed for a raunchy but sophisticated night out in St John's. Her friends were mostly non-stop talking college students, curious about me, and quizzing Maureen about her regular boyfriend, currently in college in Toronto.

"Trevor, will you write this essay for me – I need a good grade?"

"What? Are you serious?"

"Sure, everybody does it."

Eventually, so do I.

At Christmas we troop to Midnight Mass, and as a Low Church Protestant I gaze in amazement at this holy football match, the crowd buzzing, the incense swinging. "Is it always like this?" I whisper. "Sure," she laughs back at me, "not so full as this, natch, but same kinda thing".

Since I shared an apartment, the more intimate activities of our relationship were undertaken mostly in the porch or the lounge of her family home, late at night after she made a 'Club Sandwich'. We went swimming, we went to the Cinema, we went to concerts. We joined in the ex-pat social events. We lived for the moment. It was fine.

Except of course that it wasn't.

★ ★ ★

"Come on Shirt, get your socks off".

Back in the office, the British planning insurgents were getting a reputation for being unconventional at best, wild anarchists at worst. We had been dubbed "the dirty dozen". John led the way, painting a pastiche of one of St John's sprawling suburbs across the corridor walls, in an effort to show everybody how awful local housing was in terms of design and layout. In Canada "landscaping" meant that literally: bulldozing sites to strip them of all living things and building brick and concrete duplexes along long, winding tarmac roads. It was the epitome of 'sprawl', everything that good British planners and environmentalists abhorred.

My role in this new exercise was to be held sideways in the corridor with my bare feet splashed in white paint to plant footprints across this work of art, for reasons that now escape me – probably to impose some quasi-Dali surrealism onto the picture. It was great fun, and the salaried slaves of Joey's Confederation Building seemed to enjoy it too, even if they were somewhat bemused. And I have a sneaking suspicion that many of them thought the layout of the housing estate was just *booful*..

The reaction from Canada's Housing Corporation was less sanguine, especially John's proposal to put the extensive wiring that festooned urban St John's under the ground. Newfoundland is essentially made of hard rock, with not much soil. The cost would have been astronomical. This was where our planning fantasies – from John's design ideas to my structure plan theories – finally hit the deck.

Jim was much more tuned to the real needs of local communities. He was quietly getting on with the job of preparing municipal plans that delivered good water and sewerage systems, making places that were fit to live in. Meanwhile the Colonel was keeping the bureaucrats and politicians happy, whilst nurturing his new team in a wonderfully avuncular and shrewdly tolerant fashion. "I see !" was his non-committal remark to some outlandish suggestion put to him by one of the "dirty dozen". When I came to work one day in a T-shirt, unheard of in the offices of the government, he had a "quiet word" with me in the Gents, pointing out that although he didn't mind, others might be offended. He provided a calm, authoritative presence that commanded respect. Unfortunately this was less apparent for his deputy, whose panicky shout on emerging from the Colonel's office – "Heh, it's gone political !" reverberated round the offices as we all echoed his shout with grinning faces.

★ ★ ★

"Jesus in the Garden!"

It's the big fella sitting next to me on the EPA flight from St John's to Goose Bay, as the plane lurches sideways on our approach to the Labrador USAF Base. A huge cross-wind has simply shoved the plane across the runway approach. We touch and bump, buck and swerve, and finally crunch down on the tarmac. There are cheers and shouts of relief referencing mothers, Christ the Lord, and brown trousers. Later we are told that there were 50mph cross-winds and that a QuebecAir flight had turned back, prompting EPA to show them who had what it takes.

I was here to do planning, following through on my Municipal Plan (with the innovative skidoo ways) for Happy Valley, the small collection of clapboard houses and facilities that housed many of the workers at the USAF Base from the Inuit community. Geographically and technically this was a long way from St John's and the finer points of planning policy that I had been debating with my colleagues. The temperature was minus 20, but with a blue sky and a bright sun. The land looked crisp and fresh, the first page in my imaginary Biggles Annual that had lured me to this country. This is partly what I had come for.

"Good morning, Trevor, did you enjoy the flight?". Dan, the town clerk greets me with a raised eyebrow –

he has heard the story of the plane's landing already. His office is part of a modest but well furnished clapboard building in the centre of the community.

"Welcome to Happy Valley. Good to see you – we don't get many of Joey's boys out in these parts."

"Thank you, Dan. Well its new to me, of course, but I will do my best to get on with the Plan" I say.

"First thing, do you have a car that I can use to get around?"

"Sure. Well not exactly a car, but we have got the dog-catcher's truck – would that be ok?"

Well why not? That would be another first, I thought.

The dog-catcher's truck turns out to be very useful. Nearly every house in Happy Valley, each standing in its own little snowbound plot, has a fierce looking husky or two chained to it. Walking around the streets does not feel secure. Whether the huskies recognise the dog-catcher's truck and are cowed by it I cannot be sure.

Huskies in Happy Valley (taken from the Dog-Catcher's Truck …)

18

The town – or village – looks bleak, desolate, hardly a person in sight. The people are either working on the Base – "eskimos", as they were then called, had a reputation as excellent engineers, able to perceive mechanical workings in very acute ways – or presumably hunkered down in their homes. There is little sense of life outside the Municipal Office and the Hotel where I stay. "Happy Valley" seems like either an over-optimistic sales pitch or a cynical observation.

I do my surveys, talk with the council, and pitch my plan, complete with new Skidoo Ways threading through the town. They seem receptive if a little bemused. On the whole it seems to go well.

But I also have to visit the USAF Base to talk to their senior staff. Arriving at the Base Gates with Dan in his car, we hand over our papers and explain our mission. The Clerk and the soldiers exchange friendly grunts, and they take the papers. They also take a good hard look at me. They go back to their office. We can see them talking, looking over to our car. Another officer joins them. Something is wrong.

"Excuse me, sir, I'm afraid we cannot allow you on the Base with your hair like that – its longer than the regulation length."

I was dumbfounded, and must have looked it. But, what the heck, I suppose they were just living up to the American Military stereotype. What else would you expect? On the other hand I was a Canadian provincial civil servant – did they have the right to exclude my entry? I looked for help from Dan, but he was in a difficult position. He had to work with these guys, and

Happy Valley depended a good deal on American money. Also I actually thought it was rather funny. Would they cut my hair themselves?

"Sure, we can do that".

So that's what we did, and twenty minutes later I emerged with an all – American crewcut.

It was much later that I realised that I could – and probably should – have made a diplomatic incident out of it, albeit in a way that did not compromise Dan and his Happy Valley community. But at the time I did not have the political awareness, let alone the confidence, to do that. But the shock – and laughter – my shearing generated back in St John's was palpable, and may have stimulated other thoughts about the US of A.

* * *

Back in Happy Valley there was time for other diversions, such as trucking up the coast to the Grenfell Mission and meeting the people there – still in bright, freezing sunshine; skidoo-ing across the frozen wastes, and feeling scary about how far you could go so quickly, and how hard it would be to get rescued if you broke down.

I am accompanied on these jaunts by one or two people I meet at the Base. The RAF had a small presence at Goose Bay and ran a small bar and club, reputedly stocked with Watneys Red Barrel, flown over by their jets from England. Thankfully I don't find the beer, but I do find Sally, an attractive South African young woman on some kind of Labrador adventure, and Bob, a good-looking young American drafted into the Services – and trying to avoid Vietnam. They are good company, and we share long conversations about the wider world outside.

We get on well – unfortunately a bit too well. After one long skidoo ride, Sally heads back to the group she was travelling with, but Bob has got locked out of the Base – it was after curfew time. I suggest he stays at my hotel – he could share my room. But there is only one bed. Naively perhaps, thinking nothing of it, I offer him one half of the bed. After ten minutes of chatting, continuing our long conversations of the day, I realise that he has intentions that go beyond the intellectual or the platonic.

Whoa! I make it very clear to Bob that this is not what I had in mind. Fortunately, he gets the message completely. No problem. We drift off to sleep, and next morning get up and breakfast as if nothing has happened. We part good friends.

I hope that he managed to avoid Vietnam.

★ ★ ★

"Trevor, have you ever been ice skating?"

Maureen, back in St John's, is looking at me with a sly grin and a twinkle in her eye.

"Well, mmm, we once played ice hockey in the harbour when it iced up. But I've never actually worn ice skates".

"Time you did then".

We put on our thick jumpers and walk up and around Telegraph Hill. It is freezing cold, but fine and sunny. Half the youth of St John's seem to be out on the ponds,

21

playing ice hockey or just crazing around. My tottering efforts are greeted with disbelief.

"Hey mister, why can't you skate?" they shout.

"We-ell, where I come from we don't do this too much".

They race around me, thrilled to be able to beat an *adult,* and gaze at me in wondrous pity. Maureen chaperones me as best she can, but I do not see a rewarding future in this particular recreational activity.

"Maureen, I think I've had enough of this. Let's go for a walk."

I take off the skates, and we wander around the ponds, arm in arm. We are comfortable together, and I remember my Uncle Bill and Aunty Vi when I was a kid, walking along the cliff top on that holiday in Dorset, being romantic. This moment is good too, suspended on that frozen hilltop in another continent.

We wander back to the skating pond, where we left our skating kit. Just over the hill I catch the edge of some kind of emergency vehicle, and when we come into the full view of the pond, *Deadman's Pond*, we see that everybody has stopped, clustered in groups, hockey sticks held straight down, looking out to the middle of the pond. Here two wet-suited and masked divers are manoeuvring in the broken ice. The air is silent, the laughter and shouting gone. In the short time we have been away on our little romantic wander, one of the ice hockey players has crashed through the ice and, weighted down with all his kit, drowned. We stand and watch too, in disbelief. Newfoundland is showing her very raw side. Some stun, indeed.

"How come ya can`t skate ?". Incredulous Newfie youth on the presciently named Deadman`s Pond near St John`s.

★ ★ ★

Easter, and Maureen is not happy.

"You didn't send me a card". Her normally smiling face is set hard and dark.

"A card? But it's not your birthday?"

"No, not my birthday – Easter!"

"Easter?" I open my mouth but no more words came out, just a gulp and a laugh.

"OK, so you think it's funny. I don't." And with that, Maureen walks out of my apartment.

Not since Ginny slapped me round the face in the primary school playground have I been so stunned (or stun, even). But for once I didn't want to take this lying down, whether through pride or a passive acceptance of fate. I run after her down the steps of the apartment buildings.

"Maureen, I'm sorry, I didn't realise it was so important. We hardly ever give Easter cards at home".

She looks at me in disbelief, her lips lowered. But she doesn't run off.

Yet things were never quite the same again.

* * *

And I was missing England. I received a letter from one of my school footballing mates telling me that Parky had died. Parky, the languid (so languid he was nicknamed "Doze") golf playing, dart throwing, gambolling left wing soccer player and fishing chum had succumbed to a longstanding pulmonary illness. He'd had a bit of wheeze and cough for some time and complained of the cold in 'Mag's caff', the 'digs' in Wythenshawe that I had recommended to him when he came up to Manchester University after me. I hadn't thought much of it. Didn't think it was serious. Even when he was hospitalised in the summer I left England, I hadn't thought it was life threatening. Now apart from being devastated by his loss – friends didn't die at our age? – I felt remorse, a dereliction of care. I should have realised. And I remembered one comment he made when I visited him in hospital:

"When are you going to do the decent thing with Stella then?"

I had grinned sheepishly, but something in his voice sounded quieter, deeper, like your Dad or Uncle, not your mate. I should have clocked that he was going somewhere beyond the usual banter.

Memories flooded back. Fly fishing on the Lymington river, his casting so effortlessly flowing, like his darts and golf. Being chased by young heifers on the banks of the Avon as soon as he had spotted their malicious intent:

"Whoa, come on Trev, they are after us!" and his chuckling, throaty laugh when we had found safe ground.

His Dad had been an airline pilot, and very organised. Doze had those skills too, but tended to mock them, even while chiding me for my usual lack of preparedness.

"You should have full repair kits in the boot, like Dad's 'long distance car'"he would tell me, with a grin. But he was not averse to a bit of 'make do and mend' himself: on his old Rover he had fixed up a small hammer in the boot to keep tapping the fuel pump when it frequently failed, the hammer attached to a string which ran into the back seat for one of the passengers to pull when required. It was the only car I ever knew where back-seat driving was meant literally.

There were trips to play football for the school old boys, against public schools such as Clifton, Eton and Marlborough. Doze, who had boarded at the small house run by one of the masters, had picked up some of the snobbery that our old grammar school affected in such fixtures, but implicitly rejected it.

"Whass this depot, then?" he would snigger as we entered Winchester to get thrashed at cricket.

I wrote to friends, and to Mags at Manchester. I wept, and felt a long way away.

★ ★ ★

I also missed Stella very much, and England. Newfie had been an extraordinary experience, but almost unreal. And for all its diversions the idea of settling there was a non-starter. It was a great place to escape from many of the ills of urban living, but at age twenty two that wasn't my problem. I wanted some good professional experience and I felt that if I stayed too long I would find it difficult to get a good professional position elsewhere. On the one hand I had left England for a Biggles-like adventure, and for good money. On the other hand I didn't want to fall off the professional ladder – I had *some* ambitions as a planner. I even thought about doing a Masters at MIT, and sounded out some of the distinguished academics and consultants who visited Newfie on a Canadian RTPI Conference we helped organise. But that plan was predicated on not returning to England.

To say that I had not really thought all this through would be an understatement. But in the summer of 1969 I booked a flight back to London, swinging London, for my holiday. And to see Stella.

Flying over the green fields of southern England with their narrow lanes and dinky toy cars presented the shock of re-entry after the rock and scrubby trees of Newfie. And London in 1969 was on a permanent high of new music and fashion which had seemingly blown the old order apart. Stella and friends rented a flat in NW3, close to a brilliant array of pubs and shops. The atmosphere was vibrant and exciting, almost intoxicating. Fashion photographer David Bailey was hanging out in the Queens Hotel by Primrose Hill, and Joan Bakewell was drinking in the Princess of Wales in Fitzroy Square. I had money in my pocket to buy drawer-fulls of flower-power shirts and ties, and go out every night for a beer and a curry. I even hired a car to take Stella and myself on a tour of cathedrals, and go to a Cambridge Spring Ball with Stella's sister Alison (who was a student at the University) and Trevor, another old friend of Stella's.

I wanted Stella as much as ever, and asked her to join me in Newfie. I was absurdly convinced that she would come, without bothering to consider the fact that she was going out with someone else in London, or whether she could be happy moving from swinging London to an isolated island on the North American seaboard, or indeed how that would work with my new social scene there, not least my relationship with Maureen. It had all the makings of a perfect emotional storm. And when Stella agreed – reluctantly, guiltily? – to my request, that perfect storm was all set to take place.

★ ★ ★

I am waiting at Gander Airport for the incoming flight from London. I have a hired car that I have used to visit some nearby small towns on more or less spurious business visits, now ready to drive Stella back to my new apartment in St John's. I had rented an elegant clapboard 3 –bedroom maisonette, a good step up from the Lakeside apartment Jim and I had shared, and big enough to share again with him, but perhaps not surprisingly in view of my impending re-liaison with Stella, Jim had politely declined.

The plane touches down and taxies to a halt some 200 yards away on the runway. Down the steps come the passengers, slightly hesitant, each probably wrapped up in their own apprehensions and plans, stepping mechanically towards the airport buildings. One passenger has luxuriant black hair and a very white dress with a short flared skirt showing off the most fabulous legs. It is Stella, arriving from swinging London to the scrub and rocks of Newfoundland, via the white elephant of Gander. She looks terrific, and I am duly knocked out.

★ ★ ★

I wasn't the only one to be knocked out. In what passed for club night life in St John's the length of Stella's skirts attracted attention at a level way over what might be taken as flattering, both for her and, by association, for me. It must be one of the few times in my life when I experienced an impact of paparazzi proportions, albeit in a far-flung corner of eastern Canada. Stella regarded it as a matter of feminist freedom. The locals had another word for it. Either way, it reflected the huge cultural gap between London of the late 1960s and Newfoundland, already famous for its 'two-year lag'. It did not bode well for a settled existence – for either of us.

Yet my 'bosses' had been more than helpful. The Colonel and his deputy (the one I had mistaken for the social secretary) pulled strings, and helped Stella get a job with some Montreal – based consultants working on a plan for St. John's. It was another kind gesture typical of the Colonel. A cynic might judge that it may have reflected a little unconscious approval of my bringing out another Brit to join our ex-pat community, but it was by any reckoning a genuine and generous action on his part.

But it left Stella rather isolated in a small engineering office in the city, while I continued to work in Confederation Buildings with my colleagues, who were also my friends and formed most of my, and our, social life. We lived in a splendid but too-large home with half of it unfurnished. We drank at the *Tudor Inn* with its jazz and talcum – powdered floor in the evenings, and ate mono-sodium-glutomate-soaked meals at sundry Chinese restaurants. Stella had been transplanted from a culturally rich and socially dynamic environment to somewhere altogether more primitive. It did not help that I was feeling the guilt of leaving Maureen, and apprehensive of her presence in the city. All this while we were actually starting a new life together for the first time.

We had rows. At a party I had organised at our home, Stella retreated upstairs and, clearly upset by something I had said/not said or done/not done, started throwing stuff around. Everyone could hear. But I ignored her, considering her behaviour over the top. On another occasion she locked away my football kit before a big game. I had to make up some story about losing my gear. At night, we just about slept in the same bed.

There were *some* good times. Tobogganing down a nearby slope, my watching her bob-bobbing down in her dogtooth checked coat. Pic-nicking with friends on

Stella – from swinging London to rocky Newfoundland

the rocky scrub outside the city. Ridiculous attempts to make home-made beer.

There was also a memorable trip to the French islands of St Pierre/Miquelon – to play football. I had taken up playing football for the Guards, a local team in the St Johns League. Like most things in St John's (and Ireland) the teams were based on historic religious affiliations, the Guards being Protestant. They were languishing near the bottom of the local soccer league, but had taken on a bright new English player – coach to shake things up a bit. Pat Smith was from Leeds and had all the skills and discipline associated with that very successful team of the 60s and 70s. He transformed the Guards from a style that I reckon even pre-dated the 'W' formation of the Walter Winterbottom era. For example the full –backs fixed themselves into position on the corners of the penalty area and simply stepped out and 'checked' you (in ice hockey parlance) by taking you out of the game : one man-mountain picked me up by the scruff of the neck and swung me around through nearly 180 degrees – my protests to the referee were ignored. But Pat changed the Guards to a much more mobile, passing team that was something nearer the modern game. The St John's Telegram responded. Our goalkeeper was a friend of one of the reporters, who frequently headlined him, "recording the shut-out". I was delighted to read that Cherrett "put the game away for the Guards at the 23-minute mark" and "dented the twines from twenty yards". We steadily got results and moved up the table, and by the end of the season we were challenging for top position.

"Excusez-moi, je desire quatre salle de bains, s'il vous plait?". I was trying to book accommodation for a group of us going on the St Pierre footballing tour. The telephone line was difficult from St John's and I wasn't sure whether I had got the message through properly. But we went anyway, first in John's Mini along thirty miles of rock-strewn track down the Burin Peninsula, then by fishing boat to St Pierre, some 16 miles off the coast. Everybody was sea-sick, except Stella who had sensibly (as ever) taken tablets. I had been holding out by sitting still, only succumbing when one of the Guard's directors or some-such hailed me noisily and banged me on the back with cheery gusto:

"Hi Trevor, how ya doin?" he booms. I smile weakly. I feel like pushing him into the rolling sea.

We play in a delightful local stadium before a crowd of a hundred or so, not surprisingly losing the first game on the afternoon of the voyage, but coming back spiritedly to draw on the second day. I love it: the local crowd are generous in their praise, and I think they see something of a fellow spirit in my style of playing –and possibly my longer hair, in contrast to the short-cropped heads of my fellow-players. Pat reckons it is the best game I have played for the team.

The Islanders' hospitality is generous and warming. Despite my attempts to book four *bathrooms* our hosts sort out some accommodation. And for all of us it is a memorable adventure.

★ ★ ★

So my life with Stella was some way short of complete disaster. Thomas Hardy would have recognised it, I am sure. An old note book of mine mysteriously records that *When Billy Liar meets the Queen of Orpington there will be Sparks* – followed by some even more opaque prose-poetry. This is interspersed with some notes about creating new communities in northern Canada (a project that Boz and I briefly embarked on), a shopping list, and a briefing for the Colonel …

What was clear was that neither of us wanted to stay in Newfoundland much longer. We planned to travel across Canada and North America to Mexico, for the 1970 World Cup. We would leave in the Spring of that year.

To achieve this I bought a Volkswagen Variant, a small estate car in which to journey across the continent.

It was an excellent vehicle with an instant petrol –fired heater, a great advantage in the Newfie winter, and plenty of space in the back for luggage. VWs were the business here – so much more robust than the Ford Anglias and the like from England. I had inherited an ancient VW Beetle from a couple of English planners who had been working in Newfoundland before I arrived, then moved onto a Sunbeam Alpine owned by one of our Newfie friends in the office. But this turned out to be a disaster – it was always breaking down and the local garage made a right mess of a new paint job I had commissioned. I finally put the piston rods through the crankcase on the TransCanada Highway – too far from help and forcing me to stay overnight, luckily in a nearby log cabin.

So the Variant was far and away the best car that I owned in Newfoundland. But this too ended in another kind of disaster.

Early in 1970 I was driving out to visit Harbour Grace, one of my 'local plans' north –west of St John's. It was a dull, cold, but dry day when I turned off the main road for the minor road round the Bay to the town. As I swung into the road the car just kept on swinging round, utterly out of control, swerving backwards. Black ice. Before I could react the back wheel hit a rock with a bash and a bang that sickened. I was not going anywhere in this car that day, or possibly again. The only good news was that I had not been travelling along some precipitous cliff to send me to my doom.

"Hello, Stella? I'm really, really sorry. I'm in Carbonear – I've pranged the car. It was terrible, I just lost it on the ice."

My phone call to Stella was one of desperate remorse. This was my third prang in Newfie in two years. Apart from the Sunbeam I had lost the back end of a hired Plymouth Fury 3 on a snowbound hill. The big truck coming down the other way had not stopped or even slowed down – perhaps he had no choice. It was another dark moment in the icy wilderness of this island.

"It's OK. Are you sure *you* are OK? Don't worry about the car". Stella's forgiving reply comforted me.

I was towed to a garage in the nearby town of Carbonear, sitting in a shocked trance at the steering wheel like a foolish clown. Weeks, then months, followed in which this garage attempted to repair the car, complicated by the rear location of the engine – close to the gearbox differential. I journeyed out several times by bus to talk to the mechanics who assured me it would be sorted.

"Yep, yep" became a catch-line for ever after, a 'newfie' version of the Devon and Cornwall *dreckly*.

In the end they never did get it right, and we left the Variant with John to sell as best he could. We booked flights to Montreal, after which we planned to travel by train to Toronto, Chicago, St Louis, Laredo / Nuevo Laredo, and finally Mexico City. By May we were on our way.

★ ★ ★

Newfoundland had been a truly new found experience. It was so different from anywhere I had ever been – before or since. The people were extraordinarily friendly, and the shore-scape had charm – the clapboard houses, the boardwalks, the 'flakes' – the wooden platforms for drying the fish. We watched the Gadarene inrush of spawning capelin in the Spring, chased by shoals of cod. The 'white fleet' of Portuguese sailing vessels fishing the Grand Banks with their tiny dories still came into St John's Harbour. I caught sea trout in Quidi Vidi. We ate cod's tongues and seal flippers in the town restaurants.

But underneath this enticing picture lay a deceptively brutal world – the ice ponds sucking in and closing over the overburdened ice skater, the frozen roads luring cars and trucks to destruction and death. In *The Shipping News* Annie Proulx talks about "*this rock, six thousand miles of coast blind-wrapped in fog, boats threading tickles between ice-scabbed cliffs*". She also captures the sense of 'anything could happen' in this wild and neglected island :

The father who shot his oldest children and himself that the rest might live on flour scrapings; sealers crouched on an ice flow awash from their weight until one leaped into the sea; storm journeys to fetch medicines – always the wrong thing and too late for the convulsing hangashore.

We lived there in better times, in the 'soft city' of St John's, with its legacy of British colonial rule, and its inheritance of American urbanism – all highways and malls, where (Annie Proulx again):

> *Now they said that hard life was done.*
> *The forces of fate weakened by*
> *unemployment insurance,*
> *a flaring hope in offshore oil money.*
> *All was progress and possession,*
> *all shove and push. They said.*

I experienced both sides of this "wild and neglected island". And I enjoyed a great first job, many kind people, and some lifelong friends. I would not have missed it for the world.

A Newfoundland `outport`: fishing was once the staple industry

Chapter 2

To Mexico

Our first stop after leaving St John's was Montreal. It could hardly have been more different from Newfie. A big city infused with French culture, modern architecture and a contemporary buzz in the aftermath of the 1968 Olympics. A whiff of danger as the Quebecois were campaigning for independence, and occasionally blowing up post boxes on the way.

We stayed with Jean-Claud, a photographer working with the planning consultancy that had employed Stella in St John's. As part of the consultant's plan for St John's he had produced a brilliant photography exhibition that had attracted great interest amongst the locals – it had captured many aspects of life in that city, past and present. Now we saw him in his own habitat, an urban chic apartment in the historic quarter of Montreal, arguing with professional friends over coffee and croissants about urban design and politics.

It was a fleeting glimpse of a different metropolitan world. Next day we got the train to Toronto, all high-rise offices and shiny shopping centres, the capital of Canada's booming commercial growth. Anglo-Saxon rather than French. This is where Newfies came to work on the big building sites, to make money for a few months or years, then to return home.

We spent several hours trooping round the streets of Toronto, looking for shoes to replace Stella's broken heels. Like my Gran, Stella was (and is) very *particular*. But apart from its gleaming tower blocks and wonderfully clean and quiet Metro, Toronto is for me forever associated with a succession of shoe shops that failed to deliver the right shoe …

Next stop Chicago. Heavily armed police in the station foyer cast a harsher, more fearful atmosphere. Time for a quick taxi tour around the city – the highlight seemed to be the Wrigley building, "the biggest building in the world", drawled the driver out of the corner of his mouth, appropriately chewing gum.

Then back to the station for the train to St Louis, where we changed onto the *Texas Eagle,* a passenger train with just two carriages and a dining car that ran through the heart of the Mid-West, southward to the Mexican border. Even in 1969 there was something old-time about this train, with its faded seats, table-clothed dining saloon, and pedestrian pace – from the Box Car at the rear you could watch the individual timber sleepers going one by one across the tracks. To either side the cornfields stretched for ever throughout the day. The monotony was only broken by a hot chili sandwich that scorched my mouth at lunchtime. Yet there was something impressive about our slow journey through this huge continent.

Next day something *did* happen. The scenery had changed from corn to beef cattle, with a surprising amount of green fields and trees. But we didn't have too much time to take it in. A tornado had been ripping through Texas and the train was forced to stop. At Austin we were transferred to Greyhound coaches, alongside a fresh bunch of Texan passengers in big yellow flared trousers and huge white hats. At San Antonio we boarded another train to Laredo, predictably late – an hour after the timetabled connection with the *Aztec Eagle*, scheduled to leave Nuevo Laredo, just across the border, for Mexico City.

"Come on, lets get a taxi, it will probably wait" I said.

We arrived at Nuevo Laredo station to see the *Aztec Eagle* trailing off southwards down the line. It was a memorable statement of *un*integrated transport. My travel diary is cryptic: *Why couldn't the bastards wait?* Later we learnt that we had travelled on the *Texas Eagle's* last journey on that schedule.

Time to sample some Mexican cuisine in Nuevo Laredo – guacamole and tacos – and share a filthy hotel bedroom with some new companions that were to accompany us on our journey: *Las Cucurachas*.

* * *

We are walking down one of Mexico City's hundreds of streets towards our cheap hotel. A myriad shopfronts spill onto the pavement, people selling every kind of food and drink, clothes, and domestic services – all the products and services needed to sustain this huge city of (then) nearly 2 million people (nearly ten in greater Mexico). But my study of this bustling city life is deflected by an intense interest coming from all the street people in *us*, or more particularly Stella, and more particularly again the length of her skirt, or rather the lack of its length. And this interest is not expressed in a quick glance, and maybe a smirk or grimace, but long stares, interminable gazes, especially the men, who stop whatever they are doing, or mostly not doing, and just look, and look, and look. It is as if we have inverted the relationship between visitors and locals – *they* are the tourists. And there is not much we can do about it. Do we turn on them and shout at them? Gesture defiance? Plead for politeness? For the whole length of the street? It would be exhausting. Instead I try to ignore them. Pretend it isn't happening. Inwardly deplore it. Wish that maybe Stella could wear jeans …; Stella meanwhile is ignoring it too. Not only is she *particular,* she is also *determined*, determined not to allow the world to dictate what she should wear. If Newfoundland was an embarrassing mismatch, Mexico is a cultural catastrophe.

We get by. City transport is brilliantly informal, the taxis running along the main boulevards, picking you up and taking you as far as you want down that road for a peso, alongside other passengers doing the same. The traffic is predictably chaotic, and you take your life into your hands when crossing the road. So do the drivers – the English-language paper reports a motorcyclist shot by the police for riding an excessively noisy machine.

We visit the state-run pawnbroker near the cathedral, and offload a sleeping bag and some other excess clothing. Lunching in the park, I get talking to a young American.

Soon he is offering me 'magic mushrooms' – I make my excuses. We spend half a day at the superb Anthropology Museum in Chapeltepec Park, to bone up on the natural and cultural history of the country. We visit Teotihuacan, the extraordinary ancient city a coach ride away from the capital. Later we buy what we can afford at the brilliant Museum of Popular Arts.

We eat on the street, delicious chicken tacos, tamales, tostadas, tortas and goodness knows what else. But at night we get stomach pains –"Montezumah's Revenge' – sharp but fairly brief and without too many messy complications. The odd thing is that despite this warning, we cannot resist eating these delicious take-aways. We are prepared to live now and pay later.

Finally, one fine sunny morning we walk into a smart tourist agency office, and buy tickets for the World Cup, starting within a couple of weeks. They are expensive, clearly marked up for foreign visitors, and they are only for Guadalajara, the venue for England's qualifying round. But we have come a long way, and we have at least got seats for the first games.

It's a few hours on the coach to Guadalajara, and by the evening we check into a hotel that we had pre-booked in Mexico City. It is comfortable, quite smart, and seems to be home as well for some of the English team and their entourage, judging from some familiar faces at the bar. There is a cosmopolitan atmosphere. I get talking to a young journalist writing for the Economist, and an expansive Mexican business man who seems to know everything about the world. He is especially voluble about Cuba, which I have raised as an interesting example of a revolutionary approach. "It's a disaster, its economy is broken, it is being ruined !" he exclaims, his arms stretching out in a gesture of chaos, so much so that I notice the small gun holstered behind his jacket, and decide not to push my argument too far. We talk, and act out, a kind of fantasy that prevails in these kinds of situations. We are all 'away', nobody is 'home' in this hotel lounge, and we are all free to air our views and change the world, in the exciting context of a major international sporting event about to start. Later Stella spots Roger Hunt, the England striker, at the bar and sends a message down the line of drinkers asking for his autograph. "There's a piece over here wanting your signature", we hear someone call to him. "What – a *priest* wants my signature?!" comes back the reply. But Stella gets the signature of one of the least remembered but most effective member of that 1966 World Cup team – to go with George Best's, one of the world's most famous and brilliant players with the least memorable international playing record. Outside the Brazilian supporters are in fine form, keeping up a continuous samba drumming right through the night – just in case the England team harboured the odd idea that they might actually sleep.

But the start of this great international sporting event, the 1970 World Cup, is not all that exciting. We watch England play out a narrow 1-0 victory against Romania, a team that have come with a well drilled midfield and defence but little attacking ambition. First round games are often disappointing anyway, both teams cautious, wary of making silly mistakes that will undermine their chances of progression too early. But the brilliant

Brazilian team thump the Czechoslovakian side 4-1 and I manage to capture on camera the great Pele scoring, by gambling correctly that he would score directly from a free-kick just outside the penalty area. Game on!

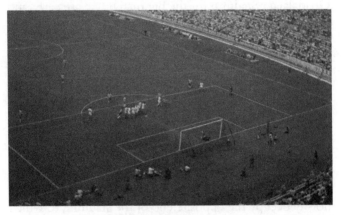

Goal !!! Pele scores from a free-kick against Czechoslovakia

The big match is next up – England, the World Cup holders, versus Brazil, the greatest exponents of the 'beautiful game'. Not only is this bound to be the highlight of this preliminary round, but there is 'history' behind it too. Alf Ramsey, England's taciturn manager, described the Argentinians as 'animals' after their quarter final match against England in the 1966 World Cup, a competition in which the great Pele had been effectively kicked out of the tournament by some of the most brutal tackling ever witnessed in international football. More recently, fuel was added to the fire by Bobby Moore, England's captain, being accused of stealing a bracelet in a Colombian shop a few weeks before the current tournament. England is not very popular in South America in June 1970.

We are soon to experience this 'history'. Naively, before the days when national patriotism will become more toxic within much of English society, I am carrying a Union Jack on a small pole as we enter the very impressive Guadalajara Stadium for the big match. We are early, and there is plenty of room. People nearby are looking at us, but not aggressively. But I hear faint whistling from around the ground, a whistling that grows louder and louder, to the point where the whole stadium seems to be whistling at us. Some people nearby laugh and point to our flag. We are feeling distinctly uncomfortable. I hold my flag modestly by my side. This could be sticky.

But our discomfort is lessened by the arrival of the main English Supporters' Club, whose flags and chanting noisily occupy the opposite end of the stadium, to which the whistling is now directed. The tension, naturally in the air anyway for this battle of the giants, could hardly have been greater. It will be a relief to get the match going.

★ ★ ★

We received a hot reception from the huge crowd of Guadalajara

And it turns out to be a very fine international football match. Not in terms of goals, or visceral excitement, but in terms of a brilliant contest fought out by two excellent teams at the top of their very different games: Brazil full of style and inventive attack, England superbly organised, playing as one unit. It is totally absorbing, and the pre-match hullabaloo is soon eclipsed. The football ebbs and flows, Brazil threatening with lightning raids by some of the finest international strikers ever seen while England build patiently to put pressure on their opponents' fragile defence. Bobby Moore plays cat-and-mouse with the great Pele, while the equally famous Bobby Charlton leads the English charge.

Two moments stand out, both at our end, where we are seated some twenty rows up behind the goal. The first inevitably involves Pele, lurking just a few yards in front of the goal, who escapes his marker and rises to head a perfect cross downwards to the beckoning net. It has to be a goal. But Gordon Banks, diving to his right, somehow scoops the ball *after* it has bounced, up and over the bar. It is a breath-taking save, and the Stadium's breath is duly taken away.

Later, Brazil do get their goal after a dazzling raid by Jairzinho, Tostau, Cesar and Pele. But with time running out substitute Jeff Astle is suddenly presented with the ball, again right in front of goal. Some-how he manages to blaze it wide – one of those horrible 'what if ' misses that haunt every striker. The chance to get a deserved equaliser has gone. Alan Ball puts a brave attempt onto and over the bar at the death, but England go down in the end. Yet not without huge courage and skill, their footballing honour intact.

The mood in the crowd is uplifted and appreciative. England have given a good account of themselves, justifying their place as world cup holders, helping to offset the view that they had only won the World Cup because of home advantage and prejudiced refereeing. Honour had been restored.

"The England match was our toughest test," said manager Mario Zagallo afterwards. "That was the real Final."

But there was a sting in the tail for me. Back on the bus I propped my flag up and out of the window. Out of the corner of my eye I spotted a youth running out of the general melee towards the coach, eyes on my flag. I hastily withdrew it as he leapt up to grab it. His hand clipped the end of the pole but I was just in time, managing to get the flag inside the window, as the coach drew away.

It had been a terrific match and I was glad that we had made the effort to get there. We were looking forward to more great contests. But it turned out to be the last time I ever saw England in a live match again.

★ ★ ★

Despite England's 1-0 defeat to Brazil, they had qualified for the quarter-finals, this time against Germany, defeated by England in that famous 1966 final in London. The game was to be in Leon, and our next challenge was to get tickets for this match. Sadly, we could not find any, not from the usual ticket selling offices anyway. We could have travelled there in hope of buying tickets at the ground, but it was a long shot and they were bound to be very expensive. We did not have a great deal of money. And we wanted to see more of Mexico.

So we travelled. Firstly, down to the Pacific coast to enjoy a bit of beach and surf at a small, half-deserted resort near Acapulco. We stayed in cheap hotels infested with cockroaches. At one we were issued with industrial sized Flit syphon sprays with which to attack the flying raiders, sometimes in the middle of the night when they buzzed the bed. The shower was riddled with smashed corpses. But by day we still ate the delicious tacos and tortas on the street – by now the stomach pains had gone. We must have been adapting to our new tropical environment.

Gone fishing, down Acapulco Way

We travelled to the distant south eastern province of Yucatan and visited the extraordinary temple of Chichen Itza, climbing the long, steep steps up to the platform at the top, the setting for human sacrifice. The raised pumping of the heart by the time the victim reached the top must have made it easier for the executioner. These monuments presented an indelible and terrible beauty.

Don't mess with us! The Aztec Jaguar is there to warn you off...

...or take the heart you sacrifice after climbing to the altar

Stella keeps her distance…

★ ★ ★

Meanwhile England were playing their quarter-final in Leon, a thousand miles to the south. That evening we ask at a bar what happened. "Si, si, Englanda win, si, si" someone says. The match is being replayed on the TV by the bar and we watch. Sure enough, England are scoring – they are two goals up! But Germany come back, 2-1. Charlton is subbed, and Bonetti fluffs a save – 2-2. Extra time, and Germany score a winner. We watch in disbelief. Perhaps our man thought England had won because Germany were wearing the white shirts. But it didn't matter – England were out of the World Cup. It was all over.

I was so deflated as we arranged to head back to Mexico city. It was a long bus ride, and we were running out of money. Our original plan to travel down to South America had long been scuppered by earthquakes in Guatemala. It was time to go home.

★ ★ ★

But Mexico hasn't quite finished with us yet. The coach is a bit of an old rattler, yet seems to be hurtling along the rumbling roads across the plain and up into the hills. I sit on the inside and can see down the central aisle to the driver and the windscreen. Round one mountain bend a lorry is coming fast the other way, too near the centre of the road. Our driver is taking evasive action, and we shift to the right, but too near the curb it seems to me. In a split second I realise that we are not going to make it.

"Christ !" I shout to Stella next to me, "get your head down!".

The coach jolts on to the verge, lurches forwards and sideways. I think "this is it".

I have no idea where we are, what lay before us. Maybe a 1000ft drop into a ravine, maybe a wall of rock. We hang on as the coach goes bumping and lurching in a crunching fairground ride down a stony gulch that seems to go on for ever. Screams as passengers are shaken and hurled into and out of seats. We keep our heads down, eyes tightened, jammed into our seats, waiting for the big crash. I remember the little wooden crosses by the sides of the road.

But the crash never comes. We slump to a stop down the gulch. Passengers are shouting and groaning, one woman has badly cut her face. The driver and his mate get the door open and help us all out. We are 50 ft below the main road, on a swathe of stony ground surrounded by gnarled trees and heather. We stand around in dazed shock, but thankful that nobody has been seriously injured.

After a long wait, a new coach comes out to pick us up. It is a bigger, newer coach, but we have lost all confidence in this form of transport. We bail out at the next town and decide to proceed by train.

★ ★ ★

The 'Mixtos' is a mixed passenger and freight train that purports to go from Yucatan to Mexico City. It has the air of what used to be called the 'stopping train' in England. Its behaviour lives up to that image and to something far beyond. Three carriages are filled with farm workers carrying a variety of belongings, including vegetables and live animals, alighting and embarking at each stop. It is very hot and humid. The toilet facilities are primitive, and the ends of each carriage smell of urine and dead chickens, which are stored in crate-like fridges, next to bottles of coca-cola or lemonade which the conductor carries down the train from time to time, shouting "Refrescos!" He always slows down when he passes us, as we gasp with thirst in the interminable heat. Not only does the train stop at every station, it often stops between them too, limping in the tropical jungle of Yucatan, waiting for some signal to move on. Worse, it will reverse down a siding, do some shunting, or simply slumber in the interminable heat.

After several hours of 'mixtos' we decide to abandon this tropical hell-train. We get off at Villahermosa, big enough we hope to offer a decent hotel to help us recover. Wearily, we hail a taxi from the station to the town.

"Lente, lente" I urge the driver as we roar off.

"Sure, sure", he smiles back.

We zoom through the red lights.

"No, *lente, lente!*", I shout, trying to explain what we have already been through that day. He smiles. Five minutes later we escape onto the streets of Villerhamosa. A modern hotel, international food. Boring, but safe. Well, not quite, the cockroaches still keep us company at night – albeit smaller, and less aggressive. When will this nightmare end?

Next day, having given up the train, we resort to another coach. The biggest, most expensive coach we can find. A nerve-wracking but comfortable, incident-free journey back to Mexico City. We learn that Edward Heath has won a shock election back in England, defeating Harold Wilson. Is there a connection with England's World Cup defeat? The world is turning upside down.

But now we just want a chance to recover from the traumas of our travelling and secure a flight home.

* * *

"Will you explain to me why this flight is so delayed?" I hear an Ulster voice at the airport check-in. It's Danny Blanchflower, the ex-Spurs and Northern Ireland footballing legend who I last saw thirteen years before, on the pitch for Spurs, being beaten 3-1 by Bournemouth in their famous FA Cup run of 1957. He is now a sportswriter for the Daily Express, and he is not happy.

We have managed to book a flight with the England World Cup entourage, at a knock down price too since some had left earlier. The Italian team are in the airport, looking very pleased with themselves, as well they might having reached the Final after a sensational victory over West Germany, and only going down to one of the greatest Brazilian teams of all time. Apart from footballers,other household names and celebrities of the day could be spotted in the queue.

But we are in no mood to celebrate or enjoy this company. Our travelling difficulties have eroded our confidence, and cast a pall over our big trip. Stella, in particular, is frazzled, and just wants to get home. Now we face a twelve hour flight, already delayed, with stops at Atlanta and Halifax, Nova Scotia. Throughout the flight she is tormented by uncertainty, the hazards of our coach and taxi trips transposed now to air transport. There is no control over it.

Eventually, finally, we fly in again over the green fields and dinky toys of England. The big trip is over. Eventful, but fraught, and challenging our partnership, our relationship. We retreat home, Stella to London, me to Hampshire. Time to recover, and perhaps to re-think.

Chapter 3

London (and Milton Keynes)

In the early summer of 1970 we were exhausted and frazzled after our marathon flight from Mexico, the trauma of the coach crash and other travel shenanigans.

Our immediate reaction was to go home to see our parents. For me it was more than that, a kind of running away from a bad experience. Not that it had all been bad, of course, but I sought the safety and refuge of my old home territory. Time for some rest and recuperation, catching up with family and friends. Hanging out down the beach, walking over Stanpit marshes, looking up old mates. Drinking down the East Close, showing up at a few parties.

It wasn't the same of course. Many of my friends had moved away, and the social glue offered by school and university holidays, football and fishing was no longer there. But it was summer time, the living *was* easy, and I didn't know what I wanted to do. I was just hiding under the soft duvet of the south coast.

I also neglected Stella. She wrote, complaining of my silence.

What were my plans?

What indeed. Stella told me that her friends Peter and Francis, part of the Pembroke holiday gang I had met in the graduation summer of 1968, were leaving their top floor flat in Maida Vale. They were emigrating to the US. It would be available in September.

It was time to decide. Were we going to resume our relationship, despite the difficulties we had experienced in Newfoundland and Mexico? I was surprised that Stella seemed to want to continue. Our year together had hardly been a great success, or even a promising start. But I still cared very much for her, and deep down I still loved her – she occupied an important part of my being. And she still appeared to want to stay with me.

I said yes, we should take the flat.

* * *

Randolph Avenue was a quietly impressive curving terrace of 18th Century 3-storey houses. Our main room was on the top floor, with a bedroom in the roof accessed by folding steps. We were lucky to have any flat in a fine part of London. Especially since we had no jobs.

Two issues had to be sorted right away – both involving sex and/or money. The first arose from something Pete had said about the fact that we were not married, and the flat was owned by the Church Commissioners. This – despite the sexual revolution of the Sixties – was a bit of a worry. Pete thought we should come clean.

We paid our rent to the Agents at an office a few streets away. I turn up one morning in my best shirt and tie to sort it out. The office is run by a slim, dark-haired woman in her 40s, who moves quickly about the room, silent apart from some quick-fire questions and answers. She does not smile. I diffidently go through the procedures for paying the rent. There is a pause – we seem to have finished.

"Oh, there is one thing", I mumble, "I should perhaps say that we are not actually married. I mean we are about to be engaged", I lie," so I just wanted to check that…."

Our landlord's agent shakes her head, turning away to her files. I don't catch exactly what she says but her face is clearly dismissing the subject as if it had never been raised. I feel very stupid and slope off, regretting that Pete had ever raised the issue.

I had form on this. Back at Manchester Stella and I had driven to Blackpool and slept overnight in the Ford Thames, on the perimeter of the Airport as it turned out. "We are sort of engaged" I had said to the copper waking us up the next morning.

The second issue was money. We were both beginning to look for 'proper' jobs in planning, but in the meantime looked to the dole for income. This turned out to be much less daunting an experience than I had imagined. I was put on some kind of 'professional register' and granted an enhanced unemployment benefit that reflected my professional (and income-earning) capability. The clerk who dealt with me was very pleasant, efficient, and respectful – he did not make me feel like a 'scrounger'. Admittedly the job opportunities on offer through the Unemployment

Benefits Office did not appeal very much. And although I was a bit worried that my two years trolling off to Newfoundland and Mexico would not look very good on my CV, I was reasonably confident that I would secure a good position in the planning world.

So there we were, in our early 20s, settled in our flat in Maida Vale, living on the dole, and applying for planning jobs. Our relationship was not entirely clear, and our working lives not determined, but there was everything to play for.

★ ★ ★

I set about applying for planning jobs. From a professional point of view it was important to re-establish myself on the career ladder after being away. There were a fair number around but not so many that looked interesting, or in places we wanted to live.

Then a mainstream county planning job came up in Hampshire, one of the leading lights in the planning world but also scene of my short-lived shenanigans as a planning student a few years before. I got an interview. I knew the main man from those times, so obviously I had not been rejected out of hand. The interview went well. I had done my homework, was keen as mustard, and although my previous experience in Newfoundland was hardly relevant to the green acres of southern England, I think they were impressed by the responsibility I had enjoyed working for the provincial government. To my delight, I was offered the job.

I was relieved that my spell abroad hadn't cut me off from the professional scene at home. Hampshire was a top planning authority, and I had done well to be offered such a good job. And it was a kind of redemption from my previously somewhat off hand behaviour at Winchester as a student.

But there was a problem. Stella was not at all excited about moving to Hampshire. London was still in her psyche, while the south coast, scene of her occasional visits to my home ground – the beaches and rivers around the New Forest – did not appeal. And where would she work?

She didn't want to go.

Tricky business, getting the right jobs for *two* people. After graduation, we had been offered jobs in Norfolk and neighbouring Suffolk, which of course *I* had buggered up by pissing off to Newfoundland. There we had managed to get her a job courtesy of my bosses' old boy network.

It was a blow. Hard to turn up such a good job offer at such a critical time – or so I thought – in my career. But in truth I was not devastated. Some of the old antipathy to Hampshire lingered in me – the feeling that it was a bit *too* good for itself, and that I would feel bound to a corporate body that would always be much bigger and stronger than me, and not give me the space to breathe, or the slack to take chances and experiment. So I told myself anyway.

They were surprised when I turned the job down, as well they might. I felt bad about it – this was no vindictive gesture on my part, far from it. It just wasn't to be.

★ ★ ★

Next up was Milton Keynes. Now this *was* exciting – a major new city to be built on thousands of acres of farmland in Buckinghamshire. The concept was new too – grid squares of roads providing flexible spaces for new houses, factories, offices and shops. No conventional town and district centres – at least in the early masterplan. More like Los Angeles than Harlow New Town. But all threaded through with a vast green linear park, aligned with the Grand Union Canal that wound its way through the site.

I was all fired up for the interview, full of planning methodology: monitoring performance against initial objectives and all that jargon arising from systems theory (and which, as it happened, later appeared to become embedded in management generally). My interviewers were senior team leaders rather than head honchos. I could see from their faces that they were a bit cynical, but on the other hand they could or would not gainsay or rubbish my offerings. I left with a feeling of inconclusiveness.

Meanwhile Stella had been offered a very interesting job with the Standing Conference of London and South East Regional Planning, or SCLSERP, a small team of intelligent, urbane and well educated planners and other professionals that provided a kind of regional advisory planning service to London and the South East Authorities. It was not a statutory body and did not have any democratic power, but it influenced thinking about the location of regional economic and residential growth, and was in fact the forerunner of the regional spatial planning body that later did plan for the region, SERPLAN. The office was in a fine old building in St James's, with The Two Chairmen pub as their local watering hole. It was a good place for a young planner to be operating, and Stella liked the people.

I now had wheels. Dad, to the rescue again, had found a lovely old maroon Wolseley 4/44, the junior version of the 6/66 police car of *Fabian of Scotland Yard* fame, seen careering out of the old London Police HQ every week on TV. With walnut dashboard and leather seats it almost matched my old Rover for iconic appeal, lacking only the stubby gear lever (the Wolseley's was a stick on the steering wheel) and the long running boards. But it was a fine car.

I was still waiting to hear from Milton Keynes. I reckoned they must have offered it to someone else and were waiting for a reply. But just as I was giving up hope an offer letter arrived. And this time the location issue didn't arise. I could (just about) commute up the M1 in my Wolseley 44. We were, once again, all set.

* * *

So by the autumn of 1970 Stella and I had, after a wavering summer, settled down in London with a comfortable flat and good jobs. What were our plans? Unexpectedly perhaps, the question was being asked by our parents. From my parents's side, it was more or less a conventional concern: living together was still regarded as "living in sin" in 1970, even if the cultural revolution of the Sixties had given it a good kicking. Dad was his usual practical self, but even he shocked me by suggesting that, given my doubts about the project – which I think he acknowledged as part of the territory – "I could always get a divorce if it didn't work out". I didn't want to countenance any such thing. Marriage would be for life.

Stella's mother's concern was more surprising. She was a highly intelligent, compassionate and free-thinking woman from a non-conformist background who certainly set no store by conventional structures or arrangements. We should do what we wanted to do. But Stella sensed that, subtly, she would welcome us getting married, all things being equal, and as long as there were no logical reasons not to. Gently, from both sides, the pressure gradually increased.

I had misgivings, given the disastrous foreign adventures, and was surprised that Stella seemed to be in favour. But we were together, we shared a view of the world, even to the extent of investing it with a shared meaning of life. We did not share a desire to start a family. Yet marriage became a default position in the absence of a strong argument against. It gradually became something we agreed to do, like choosing to go on a big trip, rather than a formal proposition. I never proposed – perhaps that had happened *de facto* in Amsterdam two years before. I did – sort of – ask Stella's mother, who enjoyed the joke.

So we booked Paddington Register Office for January 2nd 1971, and invited our immediate families to the ceremony and lunch afterwards at an excellent restaurant in Marylebone. We made a good fist of it.

No big deal: getting married in Paddington Register Office

We were in a warm and jolly mood, enough I think to provoke the Registrar to remind us of the seriousness of the event, and to enable me to be wryly amused by the sight and sound of a couple of fire engines ringing by when we emerged into the open air. We hadn't appointed a professional photographer, as is evident from the potted plant emerging from the back of my head in the one that was eventually taken.

In the evening we had a good old party in the back room of a big corner pub in Notting Hill, to which all our friends were invited from near and far. Telephone calls were received from friends in America. Old football mates showed up from Hampshire. We had a very good time.

"Good weekend?" asked a colleague in the office I worked in at Milton Keynes on the Monday morning.

"Yeah, pretty good," I said, "I got married". It took me some while to persuade them I wasn't kidding.

★ ★ ★

Milton Keynes mixed the bovine with the international avant-garde. Its offices were located in Waveney, a small village north of Bletchley, and designed in a pleasingly pastoral fashion in harmony with the surrounding countryside. Close by was the Wavendon Music Centre, home of Johnny Dankworth and Cleo Laine.

Hardly anything had been built when I arrived there. I was assigned to an Area Team covering the village of Woughton and surrounding Grid Squares. Architects, many from abroad, and technicians seemed to dominate.

I wasn't sure what I was supposed to be doing. But I was alarmed when returning from a few days' leave to find my desk had been taken apart and 're-allocated' by the technicians – for whatever purpose I never knew. They were not giving much away. The organisation being new, the normal rules did not seem to apply. A kind of pastoral anarchy held sway.

I succeeded in getting myself moved to the Central Planning Team. Mike Clegg, one of my interviewers, was the Team Leader. This was more civilised. I could see what I might be doing here. I also met a rich cast of planning characters who I remained in contact with for the rest of my career and beyond.

Mike was helpful, engaging, likeable, and made a fair attempt at rational management. I say 'attempt' because the circumstances in which he was operating were troublesome, to put it mildly. Senior management operated by grand decree from head honcho architects in uneasy collaborations with engineers, estate managers and surveyors. There was no Head of Planning, or rather the title did not confer equal status on the incumbent, a source of complaint for all of us.

But even within the team Mike had quite a posse to deal with, including a strong Welsh contingent. Chief wrangler was Len Richards, a sharp-talking, no-nonsense go-getter who had been part of the original Consultant's team – Llewellyn-Davies – who had designed the new city in the first place. So Len knew the history and the concept of the new city, and had a deep interest and commitment to many of the design concepts that were forming at this time – and later. He was also impatient, quick to see the flaws in others' arguments, and did not suffer fools gladly. Described as 'abrasive' by the Head of Planning, Len was not someone you provoked lightly. But he was also creative, stimulating and, when he had a mind to be, very generous. And he had an excellent sense of humour, even if shaded by the dark side.

Dai Edwards formed the second part of this Welsh contingent. On the face of it he was entirely opposite – or complementary – to Len: open, friendly, jocular, less 'abrasive'. But like Len, his sense of humour also ensured that nobody got away with anything; he had an instinct for smelling out bullshit and an inclination to cut down any 'tall poppies' that might be emerging. But huge fun to work with.

As Welshmen they both had an instinct for using language in a dramatic and colourful way. I often reflected on the way that they seemed to make fairly ordinary events or remarks sound exciting and amusing in a way that often escapes the English. They brought energy and humour to the whole business of work.

But not just work. Len and Dai had a passion for sailing and spent much time planning, maintaining, and yarning about boats, passages, and projects. This came home to me one day in the office when I could overhear Len, a few yards away at his desk, talking *sotto voce* but at great length and on successive occasions throughout the day to Mashfords Boatyard in Plymouth. Len and co were planning a major trip and were getting the boat up to scratch for the voyage. HQ was MK.

Jeremy Jefferies was also part of this boating club. His background was in conservation planning and he was both amusing and a very friendly and civilising influence. Likewise Gill, a junior planner in the team, and Gerry, an architect in one of the Area teams.

Len lived with his wife Vivien, a mathematics lecturer at the nearby Open University, in a splendid 18th Century Rectory in one of the villages of the embryonic city. Dai lived in a wharf house by the canal. Sometimes I would stay over and play Darts or Bar Skittles in the local village pubs. "It'll never 'appen" the old timers would growl, considering the prospects of a new city on their doorstep in the future. And walking across the village green it sometimes did seem unlikely that all this countryside would be built over.

★ ★ ★

I met another boating enthusiast at Milton Keynes. David Bucknell worked in the Community Development Department, charged with planning for the people who were going to come to the new city, as opposed to the homes they were going to live in or the jobs they were going to work at. "New Town blues" had been a headline story from the Mk 1 new towns, caused by the boredom and displacement from old neighbourhoods in London. Much sociological research theory had been directed at this issue, and as a graduate from Essex, one of the 'new' universities, Dave was in the forefront of thinking about how such problems might be tackled. But exercising those ideas in an organisation led by deterministic designers hellbent on building monuments to the conceptual fashions that guided them presented a formidable challenge.

More interesting from a personal point of view was that David lived in London and we could share the journey, at least some of the time. This gave more time to talk. Dave was part of a radical left generation that I had encountered but not really joined in Manchester. Now I learnt a great deal more, from Marx to Marcuse. It could be argued (in court, say) that I was radicalised in this period, albeit in a gentle English way. It certainly strengthened my support for the left in general, and the left of the Labour Party in particular.

David played another key part in my –and Stella's – life. Our Church Commissioners' Lease on our flat in Randolph Crescent was ending and we had to move. We found a tiny one – bedroomed flat on the second floor of a terrace in Ainger Rd, near Primrose Hill (which we shared with a small gerbil…). I loved the view down the road from the window, but space was lacking. David offered us a ground floor flat with a 'model kitchen' designed by his father, TV's first DIY expert Barry Bucknell. "Today we are going to talk about pelmets", Stella recalled from one of his programmes. He and his wife lived in nearby Belsize Park and owned some property in the area, including a garage just around the corner. The flat David was offering – at a very reasonable rent – was in Oppidans Rd, in the same house that he and his Danish wife Dorthe lived in. It was a very kind and generous offer, and we took it up. We became established residents in NW3, close to where Stella had lived after University, a skip and a jump from Primrose Hill, The Queens Hotel, and Fitzroy Square.

This move consolidated my political education, given that Dave and Dorthe were regular hosts to assorted Marxists, Socialists and fellow travellers. Living in this favoured London territory was a social and cultural education. The garden provided a relaxed arena at weekends. David kept the lawn mowed, and we shared observations of the cats chasing the squirrels, and debating whether the roof on chimney needed repairs. We could not have asked for a better landlord.

We continued to share commuting on occasion up to Milton Keynes, either in my Wolseley or in Dave's Ford saloon. Despite the attentions of his family's local garage, the Ford's croaking starter became a familiar sound outside our bedroom window. I also gave lifts to some of the architects who lived in London, mostly the international prima donnas who had descended on this golden opportunity for exercising their design talents for the public good. Occasionally they would complain about the slow speed of the Wolseley. "Tell them to get out and walk", David suggested. But one day we nearly had to do just that when oil found its way into the windscreen wipers and started smearing right across the window, just as I had taken the outside lane to overtake a lorry. I managed to edge across and limp home on the inside lane.

★ ★ ★

"Why don't you come and join us for a trip up the Thames?" It was Peter Luff, one of Stella's old chums from

Youth Club and Young Liberal days, and his wife Carolyn, who were planning to take Pete's father's 4-berth motor cruiser up river for an early summer holiday. Which is how we found ourselves at a marina in Walton-on-Thames one breezy day in June, packed for a week's cruising on the Thames. What followed was a week of total absorption, navigating one of England's finest rivers, its locks and pubs, all to the accompaniment of daily readings of J.K. Jerome's *Three Men in a Boat*. Oh, and it never stopped raining …

At Oxford we stopped at the Perch, opposite The Meadows. At Kingston Bagpuize we moored at The Trout, drinking with the lock-keeper till midnight in the gaslit, stone floored public bar. We discovered a new world.

But it still rained. At Lechlade we moored to a tree and wellied ashore to stay in the local hostelry until the floods calmed down. But we returned too soon. The crews of 20 boats moored along the bank watched as we shot through the arch at Newbridge, just escaping the side-swipe from the river Windrush pouring into the main stream. I looked back to see everybody turning back to their boats, possibly disappointed that they hadn't witnessed the boat smash of the decade.

It was another day before I realised that we were under 'reg flag' rules, ie all boats were warned not to navigate the river. Navigation rights mean by law, however, that nobody can stop you. We shot through bridges like an express train. Ignorance was boating bliss.

By Reading the flood had calmed down a bit and we survived.

Despite, or perhaps because of, the flooding, Stella and I had been hooked on boating. Exploring the river, finding out what happens round the next bend, enjoying the bankside pubs, eating and drinking aboard – it was all magic. We wanted to do it again. But not just for a holiday. We wanted our own boat.

I loved the idea, but was a bit sceptical. *Liza,* the wooden fishing boat from my Mudeford days, taught me how much work there was, and how much maintenance was required. We looked around – there were quite a lot of cheap old wooden boats, but not in great condition. There were always reasons to say no.

Then one day we saw a pretty white clinker launch with a well crafted cabin and an inboard Stuart Turner engine. Lying on the Grand Union Canal, she had been kept in great condition by a couple living in Uxbridge with a very keen boating son. The cabin was immaculately tidy and shipshape. I knew I could not say no. £395 via *Exchange & Mart.*

Our little boat turned out, we felt, to be a *he* rather than she. Named *Uchi Mata* (a judo move)we re-named him *Morgan*, after the cult film *Morgan – A Suitable Case for Treatment*, starring Vanessa Redgrave and David Warner. He – and we – were ready to go, up the cut and away to the rest of England, for the next thirty years …

★ ★ ★

I told the story of that English journey in the March 2015 edition of *Waterways World* (see pages 73-77). But in 1971 we were just starting – up the grand Union Canal to Milton Keynes. Here I could keep an eye on it after work, and take the odd trip with guests. Over the winter

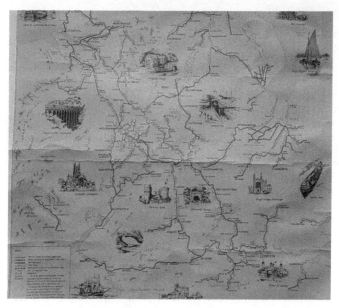

We explored most of the English (and Welsh) waterways in Morgan
Reproduced by kind permission of Lockmaster Maps
www.lockmastermaps.co.uk

I hauled her out at a boatyard in Bletchley and gave her a full fitting out with repairs to bumps and dents, seelasticating the laps between the planks to reduce leakage, and ladling on the anti-foul. It was the first of many, many labours of love in support of that little wooden hull.

★ ★ ★

But back in the office, work was hotting up. Our job was to advise on the needs of the city as a whole – recreation, shops, services and so on. The city centre was the biggest deal – how much floorspace would

Memories of Morgan

Trevor Cherrett spent 30 years navigating the UK's waterways
in a 20ft wooden boat. He recalls his many adventures...

In 1970 my girlfriend and I joined some friends on a trip up the Thames in their father's cabin cruiser. Jerome K. Jerome's *Three Men in a Boat* was our daily guide and morale booster. We needed it – it rained *every* day. We ended up moored to a tree somewhere above the bank at Lechlade, wading through the flooded fields to seek sanctuary in a hotel. Two days later we raced back down the river in our little boat, shooting through bridges, heedless of the swirling currents or the warning signs at locks. Bliss was it to be young and ignorant.

But the magic of that river journey stuck: we decided to buy a boat. I knew it would be a lot to take on – I had messed about with boats in my youth on the south coast. But when we saw this pretty 20ft white mahogany clinker boat, with a nicely fitting cabin conversion, in *Exchange & Mart* at £395, I knew there was no going back. What I didn't know then was that we would spend the next 30 years exploring the rivers and canals of England in it.

The boat was originally called *Uchi Mata*, and was moored near

Top left: Paused at St Neots en route up the Great Ouse.
Top right: Sitting pretty on the Thames

Uxbridge on the Grand Union. We decided to rechristen 'him' *Morgan* after the cult 1960s film *Morgan – A Suitable Case for Treatment*, starring David Warner and Vanessa Redgrave. It was well named, because this little boat needed a lot of treatment over the next three decades. In return, *Morgan* was to show us a completely different and delightful side to our green and pleasant land.

UP THE GRAND UNION

To start with we moored *Morgan* in London, at Cumberland Basin, near Regent's Park and Primrose Hill, where we rented a flat (impossible today!). Our first journey was on the **Regent's Canal** in 1971, where we braved the 'Pirates of the Camden Youth Centre'. However, the thought that this narrow canal connected us with the rest of the country soon had us setting off up the **Grand Union** on an altogether grander journey. This time the pirates were a bit more threatening – air guns and catapults in Southall, and shouts of "******* gypos!" at our little wooden boat (and possibly my Che Guevara beret). But soon we were making our way up the cut and through the

leafier suburbs of Rickmansworth, Berkhamsted and Tring, en route to our winter destination of Milton Keynes (where I worked at the time).

EAST ANGLIA AND THE FENS

The following year's adventure started on the **Northampton Arm** of the Grand Union in a March snowstorm, down to the **River Nene** and eastwards into a steady freezing wind from the Urals that did not stop until June. The Nene is a lovely lady of the lowland, eccentrically accessorised with stark guillotine locks, winding its lonely way around the quiet country towns and villages of Thrapstone, Oundle, and Fotheringay. Unfortunately, thanks to the elementary mistake of allowing the aft rope to get wrapped around the propshaft, we contrived to break down outside a very nasty smelling maggot factory near Rushden. Fortunately, we were saved by a very gallant engineer from the Nene River Authority who managed to hoist our boat aloft and free up the shaft. And for no charge.

On to Peterborough and the entry to the Fens. Here the uncompromising but mesmerising reed-lined channels of the **Old River Nene** and **Well**

73

Post-War Boy

| LOOKING BACK |

On the River Trent in the mid-70s.

Creek lead you straight to a tree-less horizon in a steady freezing wind. At Salter's Lode you have ten minutes on the tide to lock you into the **Great Ouse**. Miss it – as we did, of course – and you can spend the evening in a Downham Market pub where the conversation stops when you walk in. It was marvellous. Nowhere in England have I felt the land, water and people to be so distinctively different from the rest of the country.

We got through the tidal lock the next day and into the waves of the Great Ouse, blown straight down from the Wash. Through Denver Sluice and into the quiet tributaries of the **Wissey, Lark,** and **Brandon Creek**. The names alone are worthy of poetry. Instead we experienced another incident – the engine was running but the boat was apparently not. A few hours earlier we might have been carried out by the tide to the Wash. Fortunately, it turned out be no more than a loose Allen screw.

At last the weather turned warmer, as we headed south to the comfortable early summer delights of the **Cam** for Cambridge and the rowing 'bumps', then back to Ely, Huntindon and St Neots on the Great Ouse. These were leisurely weekends, driving out from London for the proverbial halcyon days on the river.

But all too soon we needed to plan a return to London – this time by trailer southwards to the River **Stort** rather than all the way back to the Grand Union. But another mishap lay in wait. Somewhere in the process of taking *Morgan* out of the water and putting him back, a plank was sprung, causing an alarming leak in the cabin. But once again help was at hand in the form of the experienced boatbuilder at Sawbridgeworth who effected an excellent repair with a skilfully riveted copper tingle.

So off we went down the delightful Stort and **Lee** rivers, back to London.

THE ROYAL RIVER

The **Thames** had inspired our boating ventures in the first place, and it continued to do so. By 1973 Stella and I had married and left London for Derbyshire. *Morgan* led the way with a stunning cruise up that lovely river in a frosty but calm and sunny March, when the trees were still just spindly silhouettes. We were almost the only boat on the river. The "season hasn't opened yet"

Top: Tackling the weed-strewn Caldon Canal circa 1975. **Above left:** Mooring at Bugsworth Basin on the Peak Forest Canal.

complained one boatyard operator when we stopped for petrol.

Later *Morgan* and its crew were to have many more happy days on this beautiful river. The Thames can often seem overcrowded, overpriced, and over-private, but there can be no denying its splendour, from source to sea.

MIDLAND JOURNEYS

At Oxford we wound our way up Brindley's **Oxford Canal** and headed north via the **Coventry** and **Trent & Mersey**. In Derbyshire we moored *Morgan* at Long Eaton on the **Erewash Canal**, handy for a major refit at Trevithick's famous old boatyard in Nottingham. He did such a good job that I gave up on a fine ex-Royal Navy four-berth pinnace I had bought to upgrade our boating experience, and we took *Morgan* eastwards down the wide, lush landscape of lonely meadows and woods of the **Trent** as far as Newark. Then we headed eastwards back along the Trent & Mersey, right through the semi-derelict potteries of Stoke-on-Trent and up the (then) recently restored but weed-festooned **Caldon Canal**; a delightful and

www.waterwaysworld.com | MARCH 2015 | **63**

74

Exploring England (and Wales) in *Morgan*

almost deserted moorland waterway, as memorable in its way as the **Macclesfield** and **Peak Forest** canals we subsequently moved on to.

Further west the classic canal experiences of the **Shropshire Union** and **Llangollen** awaited. Apart from a near-miss near Chester, when a runaway horse-drawn barge nearly took us with it, all went smoothly.

THE SEVERN AND WARWICKSHIRE AVON

Later I was to make some more ambitious south-westerly expeditions, down the **Staffs & Worcester** Canal to Stourport Basin, enjoying the convivial jostle of that historic port. *Morgan* was always at heart a river boat, and he was in his element on the **Severn** and **Avon**. But not without further incidents: a bashing from passing pleasure cruising boats while moored at the quayside in Worcester; a sinking at posh Pershore, dragged down by a neighbouring boat listing as the river level fell; and later the propshaft snapping into two parts. But all was repaired again by skilful local boat repairers, enabling a triumphant return via elegant Evesham, Shakespeare's Stratford, and then left up the **Stratford-on-Avon Canal** and Grand Union to Birmingham, memorably puttering quietly under Spaghetti Junction to the **Birmingham & Fazeley** and Coventry canals and back to the Trent & Mersey and Derbyshire.

Above right: Crossing Pontcysyllte Aqueduct hand-by-hand circa 1976.
Right: Fishing on the Upper Thames.

> "*Morgan* was always at heart a river boat, and he was in his element on the Severn and Avon"

Reproduced by kind permission of Waterways World,
www.waterwaysworld.com

be needed? The original concept of the city had been revolutionary – no big city centre, more a collection of district style centres and activities responding to needs in a flexible way – especially for the car. But this concept was totally contrary to at least two major professional and commercial interests: the architects, who wanted a big visual statement; and the estate managers, who wanted to 'peak' land values by concentrating retail outlets in one centre. No contest.

Meanwhile as planners we were charged with advising on size and scale. Architect team leaders – often several of them, such was the state of competitive team management that appeared to be fostered – would approach us and ask for our input. At first they wanted the answer immediately – preferably that afternoon! But we argued that we needed more time to prepare a more scientific calculation, based on a computer-generated 'retail gravity model' that calculated potential spending according to the location of shoppers and their distance to centres measured by size. This model – developed by and known as the Lakshmanan – Hansen Retail Gravity Model– was in essence a crude application of Newtonian physics, and could be calibrated to check it against 'real world' turnovers at retail centres in the area under study. This was all quite theoretical, and was part of a movement in planning that was attempting to embed it in systems theory, which Stella and I had witnessed in its infancy at Manchester University, notably by J. Brian McLoughlin in his 1969 ground breaking book *Urban and Regional Planning: A systems Approach* (Faber& Faber) and our very likeable and helpful studio tutor Mike Batty (*see Inset for a later research paper on this topic*).In practice, the model appeared to work quite well in predicting actual turnovers for the region around Milton Keynes[4].

As it turned out Len – my immediate boss – and Dai and Mike all disappeared on a big boating trip in the summer, and I was left to work on the model, calibrating it via painstaking successive iterations of punched cards submitted to a big central mainframe computer in the office. But it was absorbing, I enjoyed developing it, and it gave us as planners some technical credibility, however spurious.

Of course this technical calculation also depended on assumptions about the future of surrounding shopping centres. As good planners we recognised that the Bedfords, Northamptons, and of course Oxfords, all had their city centres to support and protect, and there were various regional and sub-regional planning assumptions to give context. We could not – or rather should not – go for the biggest expenditure we could muster. However, the architects, and certainly the estate agents, did not see it like that. They wanted the biggest,most humungous city centre they could imagine. The architects had photos of Paris and New York on their office walls. The estate agents were going for maximum representation by every high prestige store in the world.

Sooner or later, though, we had to put up a figure – our projected potential expenditure, and therefore

---

4   One exception was Bedford, which always seemed to perform better than the model predicted. I surmised that the 'Bedford factor' might be caused by its county town status, but I could not prove this.

by conversion the floorspace – for Milton Keynes City Centre. This was Len's job, to present our findings and recommendations to the senior team.

We settled on about 400,000 sq ft. We knew the architects wanted nearer a million. According to Len "It was like arguing with a bunch of megalomaniacs. They were completely off the wall. But we gave them something to think about".

Milton Keynes did build its million square feet in the end. And by conventional estate and design standards it was a success. To achieve this meant bussing people in

How planning tried to become more scientific: some theoretical analysis underpinning retail gravity models

Reilly's Challenge: New Laws of Retail Gravitation Which Define Systems of Central Places

M Batty

First Published February 1, 1978 | Research Article
https://doi.org/10.1068/a100185

Article information ∨

[Altmetric] 0 🔒

Abstract

This paper attempts a reformulation and generalisation of Reilly's (1931) law of retail gravitation. Reilly himself challenged workers in the field to produce new evidence which would refute or strengthen his law, and developments in spatial-interaction theory during the last decade are used here in taking up this challenge. A critique of Reilly's law sets the scene: By adopting a gravity model more general than the Newtonian model used by Reilly, it is shown how the limitations of the law with respect to hierarchy, spatial competition, locational size, and the symmetry of trade flows, are overcome. In particular the notion of Reilly's law as a special case of the market-area analysis originating from Fetter (1924) and Hotelling (1929) is demonstrated in terms of a theory of the breakpoint implying spatial price–cost indifference. Another approach, through entropy-maximisation and its dual problem, leads to similar conclusions with regard to prices, and it also serves to introduce multicentred spatial competition. These ideas are then generalised in several ways: through notions about the influence of prior spatial information, through concepts of consumer as well as producer market areas or fields, and through the implications of the analysis for the family of spatial-interaction models. A speculation on the relationship of price differentials to Tobler's (1975) interaction winds is made, and the paper is concluded with an application of these models to the definition of an urban hierarchy in the Reading subregion.

from throughout the South East and beyond. Whether that represented a sustainable retail planning strategy is another matter.

* * *

Milton Keynes may have been chaotic but it was exciting, professionally and socially. By 1972 Stella and I had settled in Dave's family flat in NW3, I was commuting up to MK (and sometimes staying overnight), and come the Spring we were underway on *Morgan*, exploring the rivers and canals of East Anglia. In March we were slipping down the Northampton Arm of the Grand Union Canal in a light snowstorm. In April we were on to the Nene, a quintessentially lowland river, a green and serene landscape punctuated at intervals by vertical guillotine locks. It was still cold with a steady easterly wind.

We also experienced the first of many 'incidents' that interrupted our progress. Leaving a lock, a loose stern rope fouled the prop, jamming the engine. There was no way of releasing the rope other than getting under the rudder. It was Easter and difficult to get help. We decided to abandon ship, mooring it on a muddy bank just below the lock. The whole area stank – just downstream there was a large waterside building that turned out to be breeding maggots in industrial quantities for fishing – *gentles* and *casters* in the language of anglers. At least we would be able to find the location easily.

On return, we found that the cabin had been broken into, and binoculars stolen. But no more damage to the boat. We sought help from some Water Authority engineers who were working nearby on the navigation system. We were in luck : a friendly foreman arranged to haul *Morgan* up at their depot and free the jammed rope – job done within the day and no payment required.

We continued on our way, through Peterborough and onto the Fens proper – *The Middle Level Navigations*. Narrow 'drains' that stretched as far ahead as the eye could see. Shallow water in which you could see shoals of bream, roach and the odd marauding pike. Reedbeds and flat acres of fen. One or two proper villages curving along the bank – *March, Upwell, Outwell* – but mostly tiny groups of houses perched by the waterway. Horizons wherever you looked, with sunsets to match. Boring? Not a bit of it, a fascinating and unforgettably unique landscape.

At *Salters Lode* you have to wait for the tidal lock to get you off the Fens and onto the open waters of the river Ouse, flowing north straight into the Wash. Upstream is the major manned lock at Denver Sluice which takes you through and on to Ely and Cambridge. Sods Law means that we just miss the Salters Lode lock opening (it lasts about 5-10 minutes) and have to wait overnight. We manage to get to a pub in Downham Market. Everybody stares as we shuffle into the bar. We eat warm pies on an old wooden table, alone. But overnight it's cold in Morgan's little cabin.

Next morning I am all tensed up to prepare the boat for our exit through the tidal lock, anxious to get the engine running properly when the moment comes. The lock-keeper emerges, gives us a look. We wait. Not wishing to leave the boat, I can't tell where the tide has

reached in the river on the other side. We wait some
more. Then, movement from the lock-keeper, the gates
open, he waves us in. In a few minutes we are out the
other side, into the wind-blown waves of the big river
(actually the New Bedford river, a kind of canalised
version of the Great Ouse) heading upstream as fast
as we can towards Denver Sluice. We definitely do not
want to be swept downstream to the Wash …

Through Denver Sluice, a huge commercial lock by
the standards we were used to, and we enter the quiet
waters of the River Great Ouse proper, soon to turn west
up the pretty little river Wissey. A gentle ripple marks the
channel, flanked by glassy reaches. Out of the corner of
your eye you can catch the odd plop of a water vole. A
Water Rail scuttles in the sedge-lined banks.

Ten minutes later the engine is running but the
boat is not. Confusion, consternation. We drift to a
standstill in the bankside reeds. At least it is idyllically
quiet. Twenty minutes earlier and we would have been
sweeping northwards with the wind and the tide and the
current out to the Wash, out to sea.

I lift the engine box lid and grub around. I prise up
the floorboards and check the propeller shaft. Then I
discover it – a loose grub screw connecting the propeller
shaft coupling to the engine. The engine was simply
not turning the propeller shaft. A quick few turns with
an Allen Key and we are back in business, at least until
we can get *Morgan* to a proper boatyard for a permanent
repair.

I was gradually building up my skills as Chief
Engineer. So far this had mainly comprised keeping

81

the one sparking plug on the two-stroke Stuart Turner engine clean, and occasionally adjusting the carburettor. Mostly the engine ran well, but now and again the petrol/oil mix would block. In extreme cases this would call for blowing down the petrol filler cap on the front deck, through a handkerchief, to get the fuel moving. You also had to watch for blockages in the water cooling system, which pumped water around the engine by a pipe connected via a valve to the water outside through the bottom of the hull. This inlet would often fall foul of weed and plastic bags, especially in shallow canals. I would regularly step back from the wheel in the open foredeck and look round the cabin door to make sure that the engine was not getting too hot. If the prop fouled it meant leaning over the aft deck and pulling out the offending stuff behind the rudder.

Now we were heading south on the Great Ouse, exploring its western tributaries – the Little Ouse and the Lark. But it was still bitterly cold in May – the wind from the east was relentless. By now I had swapped the ailing Wolseley for Dad's immaculate cream Vauxhall Victor, with seats in which you almost sank out of sight, to take us on our weekend trips to *Morgan*. Gradually the summer arrived, as we cruised into Ely, down the Cam to Cambridge for the rowing 'bumps', and on to Huntingdon and St Neots on the Great Ouse. *Morgan* was very comfortable on the river – his trim clinker hull slid beautifully through the light waves of these bigger rivers. He was in his element.

★ ★ ★

Back in NW3 we were well settled. Visitors were frequent – our London location was especially attractive to friends – and friends of friends – from Canada, where many of the 'Pembroke holiday' gang were still residing, and old colleagues from Newfoundland. My 'radicalisation' with David and his friends continued. The Conservatives were still in power after the shock victory by Ted Heath in 1970, but the 'counter-culture' was thriving, with OZ magazine on trial in 1971 for: *Conspiring to corrupt the liege subjects of her Majesty the Queen by Raising in their minds inordinate and lustful desires.*

The Establishment did not appear to have moved much further than at the trial of *Lady Chatterley's Lover* in 1960, when the prosecuting counsel Mervyn Griffith Jones asked the jury to consider: *Is it a book that you would even wish your wife and servants to read?*

What turned out to be more far-reaching was Germaine Greer's *The Female Eunuch* in 1970, which called for a revolution in women's personal lives and attitudes, not just in legislation. The Women's Liberation Movement was born, and profoundly influenced the decades that followed.

At the same time there were very politically disturbing activities: the Angry Brigade, responsible for bombing the home of the Secretary of State, Robert Carr; their counterparts in Germany – the Baader-Meinhof group; in Italy – the Red Brigades; and in the USA – the Weathermen. On a different and altogether more deep-rooted level of sectarian conflict The Troubles in Northern Ireland were now affecting England, with regular bombings and atrocities in

London and elsewhere. The hopeful and optimistic revolution of the Sixties was giving way to something much darker.

Then, closer to home, there was Bob. A friend of our friends in Canada, Bob came to stay with us on his return to the UK, just for a while to find his feet we thought. Bob was a politically radical ex-Essex student from Northern Ireland. He was good-looking, loquacious and liked football. We spent many evenings punting a ball around Primrose Hill and radically putting the world to rights. He got a job in a pub in the West End, but fell out with his employers and started a campaign protesting about their mis-use of *ullage*, the beer slops which he claimed were tipped back into the barrels. He was an angry young man. He was also a poor one and spent many hours on our phone talking to his mother in Northern Ireland. He stayed for several weeks and showed no sign of 'moving on'.

"When is he going to go?" Stella asked me, several times.

"I dunno" I said. I enjoyed playing football with him, and found him interesting company. I wasn't too bothered about him not paying any rent, or even his phone bills.

Then he ate my cheese.

It was a little *bonbel*, which I kept in the fridge for occasional snacks. I loved cheese, and was a bit put out when I saw that he had attacked it, leaving a small wedge loosely in its ripped packet. The bonbel had become a bombshell. To be fair, he could not have realised how important this piece of cheese was to me. Nevertheless, it began to symbolise for me his attitude: he was acting as guest with no obligation to pay his way.

"You will have to say something to him, Trev, he's not going to leave unless we tell him", said Stella.

"Mmm, I guess so", I murmured.

The days went by. At last I decided to have it out with him, one Saturday morning. Stella was in the garden with Dave. They knew what I had planned, and I knew they were keeping a sly eye on the kitchen, where I planned my confrontation. I sensed this so vividly that I now view this scene *from the garden*, with Bob and I silhouetted in head-to-head discussion in the kitchen window. It was painful, embarrassing. I made it as plain as I could that we couldn't put him up for ever.

"Sure, the ranks are closing, as usual", he said bitterly. I took this as a reference to his leaving our friends in Canada. But he got the message and left within a few days. We never saw him again.

★ ★ ★

There was unrest, too, in the Central Planning Team in Milton Keynes. The lack of Chief Officer status for Planning, as we saw it, provoked rebellion. Mike, as Team Leader, fought the team's case but wasn't getting anywhere with the Chief Executive or any of the other Chief Officers. Eventually he wrote to the Chairman of the Development Corporation. It was all coming to a head.

Meanwhile there was trouble brewing anyway at senior management level. There was concern that building progress, especially on housing, was too slow. Too much time was being spent on fancy design exercises, it was alleged. The Chief Executive summoned all staff to his office. His conclusion was succinct. "If you don't get your bloody fingers out, I'll bring in Barratt's" he told his stunned professional staff. The message could not have been clearer.

But our call for more powerful planning representation fell on very stony ground. Mike Clegg was moved from Central Planning to an Area Team.

"Knife in the back", growled David, as we drove home from the office. For Len and Dai, and Jeremy, who were planning a big sailing trip in any case, it was the beginning of the end. I was kindly invited to go with them but having recently married, it wasn't really an option. But I started looking for other jobs.

★ ★ ★

A couple of opportunities arose in London. The first was with the Lea Valley Regional Park, a collaboration of local authorities and other bodies that had come together to promote and develop recreation and conservation along and around the Lea and Stort Valleys, northwards from the Thames. It was an attractive prospect, well in tune with my new passion for boating (*Morgan* was now just a little way north of this area). But it was a little way off 'mainstream' planning, and might 'type-cast' me for the future. Mike Clegg, perhaps influenced by recent events that had affected him seriously at Milton Keynes, advised me against:

"As a Regional Park, it lacks proper authority or funding; it would be run at the whim of individual councils."

The other runner was the London Borough of Lambeth. They wanted a development planner, with particular skills in retail planning. They had a retail gravity model that needed developing and operating. It seemed like a shoe-in.

And so it was. I was interviewed solely by the Head of Development Plan, a genial ex-Draughtsman from the old London County Council. It was a 'mainstream' planning job that I thought would stand me in good stead. It was a senior post with a better salary. I forgot about the Regional Park, and accepted Lambeth's offer. I would now be a regular commuter on the Northern Line from Chalk Farm to Clapham South.

★ ★ ★

By the end of the summer of 1972 we needed to make plans for *Morgan*. He was having a great time on the Ouse and Cam, but I thought it best if we got him back to London for the winter. This meant lifting him out at Huntingdon and trailing him south to the Stort at Sawbridgeworth, and thence to the Lea and south to London.

The first inclination that this manoeuvre might go wrong is when I hear a muffled crack as Morgan is being pulled out of the river on its trailer. A wooden clinker boat is not well suited to such an operation, nor to the bumping along hard roads. Especially an old boat, with clinker planks much worn over time, and pulling at the seams. When he is put into the water at a boatyard in Sawbridgeworth, the truth is revealed. He has sprung a leak along one of the planks. Incident no 3 in what turned out to be a lifetime of 'incidents'. Fortunately our man at the boatyard is helpful, kindly and practical. He presses the planks down with a mop jammed against the cabin ceiling to prevent further immediate leakage, and effects an excellent repair in due course with a 'tingle' of copper riveted into the planks and sealed with seelastic. *Morgan* survives, again proving to be a "suitable case for treatment".

The Stort is a very pretty river navigation, again just right for our little boat. We soon get onto the Lea and down to the more industrial canalised sections of Tottenham and Hackney Marshes. Then west along the Regent's Canal to Shoreditch, Camden and Regent's Park, with a mooring in Cumberland Basin, just a short walk from our flat in Primrose Hill. Perfect !

* * *

We made regular family visits during our time in London. Stella's sister Christine and brother-in-law Mike lived in Beckenham with their two children Glen and Luci. They were wonderfully kind and generous hosts, and I loved seeing them, sometimes staying overnight. Chris had studied domestic science at the prestigious Edinburgh college, and her cooking was top-notch. But she was also wonderfully warm, empathetic and loving to us, Mike was extremely generous and welcoming, and Glen and

Luci were delightful and engaging children. Of course mine was an 'outside' view, but they appeared to me to be a 'model family', everything I felt my own childhood family lacked. They redeemed my jaundiced view of the 'nuclear family.'

We visited our parents too. Stella's mother had moved to a very pleasant flat in Cambridge and she was always a most generous and welcoming host. Occasionally we would venture down to Bournemouth to see my parents, and again they were delighted to see us. Dad especially warmed to Stella. He saw and appreciated her qualities of modesty, intelligence and perceptiveness.

By now I had sold the Vauxhall, mainly because I felt guilty about messing it up where it was parked in the street below the trees, dropping leaves, sap and bird-shit onto its shining bonnet. But also because we didn't really need a car in London, and it would save money. It would be cheaper to hire taxis.

But by the end of the year we were getting restless in London. Lambeth had turned out to be, more or less, a disaster. The Development Plan Group was not effective, run as it was by a technician out of his professional depth. His management style was paranoid, trying to confine his staff to their desks and preventing as far as possible any contact with the rest of the organisation. The retail gravity model I had inherited was in a poor technical state, and I was increasingly sceptical about its use in a dense urban environment. But I didn't have the sense or the experience to work out how to move things forward. Meanwhile, Lambeth Borough was under increasing attack for imposing high rise blocks on a recalcitrant population. I tried to make positive links with staff internally, but for the most part they were either too cowed and inexperienced, or had by their own honest admission too much at stake in terms of families and mortgages. So I made increasing links with outside community groups, seeing myself as some kind of "bureaucratic guerrilla", influenced as I was by a growing community planning movement rebelling against much mainstream planning policy. But living on the other side of London I couldn't or didn't put in the time and care to make that kind of support really work. So I could not see much future working in Lambeth.

At the same time Stella was becoming increasingly disillusioned with 'strategic planning'. Endless studies and reports, advisory committees and meetings were taking their toll. She liked the people she worked with, and London was congenial in many ways, but she was turning away from it. So much so that she was looking for a much simpler life and indulged in alternative fantasies: keeping a lock for example, or being a postie.

★ ★ ★

When a planning job came up in Derbyshire, we both studied the map of the Peak District, the Derwent Valley and the Cromford Canal with great interest. I travelled up to Matlock for an interview, in the old Smedley's Hydro at the top of the hill. I was confident, almost cocky. It was another senior development plan post. The Chief Planning Officer, Harry Cowley, looked a bit stern and a bit sceptical. Tom Knuckie, the Assistant Chief in charge of strategic planning, was more engaging, and we warmed to each other a bit.

I was offered the job. We liked the look of Derbyshire, a bit off the track but loads of interesting and beautiful countryside. We might get a mortgage from the GLC, who were still encouraging people to leave London. We could take *Morgan* up north, via the Thames and the canals. It would be an exciting new adventure. I accepted the offer.

I didn't particularly want to leave London, especially the delights of NW3, our good friends Dave and Dorthe, and our wonderful garden flat. A few tears slipped down Stella's cheek when she said goodbye to the resident black and white cat. But we were happy to venture north to Derbyshire.

Chapter 4

Derbyshire

On a still, clear day in March the river Thames looks wonderful from the bow of a boat moving through its calm waters. The trees are still wintery skeletons, and the bankside sedges brown and yellow, mirrored in the flat glass of the river. The sky is blue, the air is cold, but the sun is shining. And best of all, the river is deserted.

So *Morgan* has the Thames to himself when we make our journey northwards from London, this time out of Brentford from the Regents Canal into the tidal reach to Teddington, then on through the opulent London suburbs of Kingston, Sunbury and Chertsey to the western outposts of Maidenhead, Marlow and Henley.

Getting petrol for the Stuart Turner is a bit of a problem. "The season hasn't started yet", says the lady at one boatyard, kindly filling up our cans nevertheless.

At Henley's famous Hobbs boathouse, a man in blue overalls looks closely at *Morgan* as we approach. "I know that boat", he calls. He proves it too, describing a small instruction notice screwed into the side of the front cabin. "It ended up on one of those islands", he says pointing down the river, "and that Stuart Turner has been dried out more times than I've had hot dinners".

This alarming story was the first – and as it turned out – the last time that *Morgan's* history came to light from any personal recollection. With hindsight, we should have pressed him further. But we had to get on.

And on we went, in splendid mid-river isolation, savouring the vistas of this gloriously opulent waterway in its middle reaches. At Wallingford there was ice on the deck in the morning. At Abingdon we stopped for tea. And at Oxford we departed the Thames for Brindley's narrow winding Oxford Canal, northwards to Banbury and Rugby. David – disoriented from his usual metropolitan habitat – and Dorthe joined us for the Coventry Canal, on to Fradley Junction and the Trent & Mersey, and then eastwards to Burton-on-Trent and Derby, *Morgan's* new home.

Up the Thames in March

★ ★ ★

Morgan's journey took several weeks. In between times we were moving to a semi-detached house on an estate in Chesterfield, courtesy of Derbyshire County Council who had compulsorily purchased it to make way for a new ring road and offered it to us for temporary accommodation. It had three bedrooms, and a pit in the garage for repairing your car. The pit was impressive but sadly redundant for us. I enjoyed telling Dad about it though. And our new home was also convenient for Stella, as she had got a job in the Derbyshire Area Planning Office in Chesterfield.

Meanwhile we searched for somewhere to live near Matlock, in what we regarded as the more beautiful landscapes of the White Peak, adjoining the Peak District National Park. The first Estate Agent's office we entered in Matlock had just received notice of a cottage for sale in Bonsall, an old lead-mining village in the hills above Matlock. We went to visit.

This meant a journey through this distinctive historic landscape of limestone hills and valleys with it's mills, factories and water power installations of the early industrial revolution. Through the inland resort of Matlock Bath, right at Cromford for Arkwright's mills, then up the *'jelly'* (the Via Gellia) to the *Pig 'O' Lead*, bearing right up steep *Clatterway* to the village of Bonsall, planted in jumbled terraces around one of the many hills on the edge of Bonsall Moor, DH Lawrence's 'top of the world'.

Like *Morgan*, it was love at first sight – at least for me. *Hazelnut Cottage* was a two-up, two down stone –

rubbled house at the near end of a tiny terrace of three at the top of *Arter Hill*, a short but steep narrow road that climbed up from the *Barley Mow,* one of Bonsall's three pubs. It had a smashing view across and south-westwards down the valley. At the back a footpath climbed over the dry stone walled hill to the centre of the village, a small square with a pub, a post office and a butcher (with its own abbatoir). The cottage had a decent sized garden to the side, and a parking space off the little road. Perfect.

Well, not quite. The kitchen was limited to a short, narrow corridor facing the back of the cottage. But we didn't worry too much about that then.

As it happened the seller worked as a planner with Derbyshire County Council but had got a new job in the North East. He and his wife were chatty, friendly. Encouragingly, they wanted to sell to people living and working in the area rather than as a holiday home. Discouragingly, they were going to sell by 'Dutch Auction' – blind bidding – rather than accepting straight offers. That meant guessing what would be a winning figure. And lining up our GLC mortgage.

We were keen to buy and offered as high a figure as we though reasonable – £6,150. House price inflation was beginning to take off in the early 70s, and figures like this were already setting tongues wagging in the area. We crossed fingers and waited.

★ ★ ★

The County Planning Offices occupied the rambling, gloomy rooms of the old Matlock Hydro, purpose built as a Victorian Spa retreat for treating gammy legs and anything else no longer functioning properly. Fine gardens spread down the hill westwards. Some might have argued that this was an appropriate location for bureaucrats not quite in touch with reality. Especially for 'strategic planners', grappling with theoretical concepts of growth and change. My first assignment was to join the 'Mansfield/Alfreton Growth Zone' team, staffed jointly by planners from Derbyshire and Nottinghamshire, based in Mansfield. I did wonder if this was a bit of a hospital pass, taking me away from HQ on a mission that was already looking less feasible in the context of a struggling national economy – struck by the oil crisis precipitated by the Yom Kippur war and the resulting reduction in oil supplies from the Arab OPEC countries. I raised my concerns with my genial and experienced team leader, Mike Kennedy (himself the son of a former County Planning Officer for Rutland) – to little avail, and probably not making myself very popular in the process.

Most of the staff in the 'structure plan' team were youngish and male, professionally ambitious. Clive Betts, who later became a prominent Labour MP, stood out for his articulate analysis of issues. Another character stood out through his non-stop harangues in the coffee break, pinning you against the wall as others slipped away. His knowledge was encyclopaedic and his intentions worthy – unfortunately he could not contain them. Our boss, whose office I had worked in at Hampshire as a student, had didactic views and an abrasive style that was difficult to engage with. "What do you mean?" was his favourite question, expressed in almost disbelieving aggression. But he knew his stuff and kept us on our toes. And – whether intended or not – he strengthened the esprit de corps of the troops at their desks. Out of the office and in the pub he was as genial and friendly as could be.

But these were early days. All was soon to change, after the re-organisation of local government in 1974.

★ ★ ★

We were lucky. Our bid for *Hazelnut Cottage* had succeeded. Ours wasn't the highest bid, but the highest bidder worked a long way away and they were suspicious. We were bona fide local workers – and very grateful for their positive discrimination.

My old schoolfriend Richard from Christchurch kindly helped us move in. We drank in the Barley Mow to old World War 1 songs, late into the night with local old-timers. One of these was George, smoker of Capston's Full Strength and a veteran pigeon fancier, full of stories either true or made-up – we didn't know or care. Dominoes were the game of choice in the two tiny bars. Like much of Derbyshire, the Barley Mow had its own distinctive history and ways of doing things, and a warm but honest friendliness that was very attractive to us as southern incomers. It was like a backwater off a side-stream from the main current of English life.

I played football for Bonsall 'Youth' – a word that denotes any age in this part of Derbyshire and Nottinghamshire. 'Roughy' Moore, one of the Barley Mow's old-timers (he lived opposite) and a robust supporter of the team (so

Up hill and down dale: the view of and from Hazelnut Cottage

robust he was frequently 'sent off' from the touchline for abuse) had put me on to it. My selection was also inadvertently boosted by my claim to have played for Everton Youth – my explanation that this Everton was a village in the New Forest had somehow got lost …

Bonsall Youth had two pitches to choose from – one on the hill behind our cottage, which sloped away to one side so that if you played on the wing you actually lost sight of the rest of the game; and the other on the hill opposite, which sagged in the middle like an old mattress. For both of them you changed in the outside toilets of the Barley Mow. The football was hard and fast, and tricky to play on these rough hillsides. But there were some good players in the team. One was outstanding, a young 'inside forward' (in old money) fast with brilliant footwork, who would have shone anywhere. I did my best, even scoring rather flukily when the opposing goalkeeper seemed to melt away as I trundled forward. But it was hard, and I admired not only the team's skill and endeavour, but also its courage and team spirit – highlighted one day in an away match against a top – and very fit – Miners' Welfare side: not much was said, but every man in the team fought side by side and gave all to win a well deserved draw against such strong opposition. It may be a cliché, but it was a humbling privilege to play on that day in such a spirited team.

★ ★ ★

The Royal Commission on Local Government in England, which sat from 1966 to 1969, recommended the creation of much bigger all-purpose unitary authorities in what became known as the Redcliffe-Maud report. But Ted Heath's Tory Government rejected this proposal, based as it was on a thorough analysis of the best way to effectively plan and administer local government in geographically coherent areas, and replaced it by a two-tier structure of Counties and Districts. I was amongst those who thought this proposal comprised the worst of both worlds. Most Counties were not geographically delineated in a way which made sense in terms of strategic planning – Derbyshire for example stretched across several regions on the fringes of Manchester (North West), Sheffield (North), and Nottingham (East Midlands), with the Peak District National Park in the middle – while the new Districts, usually comprising several market towns and surrounding villages, were too large to operate on a local neighbourhood scale. But the proposed demise of the Shires[5] did not go down well with the Tories. Not for the first time political expediency trumped rational thinking. And it led to decades of confusion and failure in local governance which remains to this day.

But in 1974 it also created new local authorities – and jobs. It was an employment bonanza for the planners working in Derbyshire and its Area offices. Mike Kennedy became the youngest ever Chief Officer when he took over the new Chesterfield planning office at the age of 30. Another six new districts were recruiting development

5   It must also be admitted that shire counties, conceived in
     Anglo-Saxon times, still have huge resonance in terms of
     identifying where you come from

planners to prepare the new Local Plans established in the reform of plan – making undertaken in 1970, and development 'controllers' responsible for dealing with day-to-day planning applications. Meanwhile the County was creating a new Structure Plan Group to undertake 'strategic' planning, plus specialist sections dealing with transport, recreation, minerals, and conservation, with a total staff of well over 100. It was the high water mark for post war English planning.

And it meant promotion for me. As the senior planner in my team I was in a good position to win a Team Leader post in the new set-up, and I found myself responsible for an eclectic mix of topics in the new Structure Plan Group: retail planning, public participation, and the strategic implications for the Erewash Valley. Peter White, an experienced pro from Hampshire planning days, was the Group Leader, and four teams sat in bays along the old hydro changing rooms. We were an earnest lot: Chris Elton was a deep thinking economist responsible for employment policies and always ready to challenge orthodox views; Dave King was a brilliant and highly conscientious analyst in charge of population and household forecasts, in many ways the foundation for generating structure plan policies. Peter Weston was an older hand heading up the Recreation team, hugely experienced and more circumspect about what we could achieve. For my part, I brought my technical experience in retail planning, but more importantly (for me) a belief and commitment to greater public involvement in planning, informed in part from my fleeting activities as a 'bureaucratic guerrilla' in Lambeth.

Stella got a new job in the County set-up as well, joining a new Monitoring & Intelligence Group located in the same office. We were at opposite ends of the office, so rarely saw each other. She kept her maiden name of course, and many, perhaps most, did not realise that we were married.

There was an influx of new people. In my team Bill was a former journalist from Scotland, Margaret a trainee planner from Liverpool, and Pam a recent graduate from London. Bright new graduates came later from Oxford Poly, the bright new star in the planning education firmament, bringing new ideas and new lifestyles. I felt that little pang of jealousy that you might feel when you are no longer the new kid on the block. Like I had probably been, they could be a little patronising about the local Derbyshire lads and lasses in the office. But it was boomtime for planning.

* * *

So by 1974 Stella and I were well settled in our new home and our new jobs. We got on well with our immediate neighbours – Tizzy, a quiet-ish ageing lady next door in the one-up, one down; old Mrs Hardy in one part of the semi-detached terrace house beyond, a great yarner about the area and its people ("I don't like all these trees" she told us, baffling us by her perception of the landscape) and mother to the Hardy family living next door to her; he worked in a nearby builders yard, she in one of the mills in Matlock Bath – apparent from her very loud voice, often useful deployed calling to her relations living on the other side of the valley. The Hardys, with their son Gordon, were salts of the earth – and big players in the local pigeon racing scene. They had lofts behind their house, and were frequent winners cited in the local paper.

Half way down the hill lived Dorinda and her family: a big truck driving husband, rarely seen, and a young boy and a small girl. Dorinda had what might be called a big personality. She could often be heard shouting at her family, and we had a number of run-ins. Driving down the narrow hill meant passing very close to her front door, so great care was needed – especially when reversing as you sometimes had to do. But her anger seemed irrational. We tried to deal with it by 'assertive' behaviour, keeping calm and trying to identify the real problem. This seemed to make it worse. One day she came up to the cottage and started to harangue me about something or other. This was too much and I bawled her off the premises. What I thought would lead to all out war in fact led to a rapprochement. I think that this change was caused not by fear of my reprisals (force meeting force) but the fact that she had aroused my anger – I was a normal human after all. She never bothered us again.

John and Muff lived in a lovely old farmhouse just over the other side of our valley. They were both refugees from higher education and ran the small farm and woodworking operation. John made us some fine pine tables, and cleared our loft of woodworm – a very nasty job. With the price of commodities rising in the inflationary 1970s I invested in timber with him, only to find the price dropped soon after – a cautionary tale…

We decided to build a proper kitchen to replace the 'lean-to' at the back of the cottage. We consulted architects, historic buildings advisors, and local builders, in order to construct something attractive and in keeping with the cottage and its landscape. We drew up plans and took on a local builder. It meant digging out foundations at the side and rear and bringing in materials by dumper truck. We got help for the former from friends at work, pick-axing and shovelling out the earth. For the latter I hired a dumper truck to bring up the bricks and slates via the hill and a track which entered the field at the back. It was a slow and painstaking process. At one point I clipped the edge of Dorinda's cottage, but her husband made light of it in the new d'entente cordiale. But by the end of the day the diesel fumes had got to me and I collapsed in bed, a retching heap, leaving Stella and friends to enjoy their supper.

The new kitchen was a success, fitting harmoniously into the scene. Old friends from London and Dorset, even Newfoundland, came to stay, walking miles across the stone-walled fields and villages around Bonsall Moor. Our parents came too – Mum and Dad loved it, so too did Ken and Mary and the children. I loved the village, the landscape, and my work. Derbyshire could not have worked out much better.

★ ★ ★

Although Derbyshire had now absorbed our lives, *Morgan* was not neglected. We embarked on a journey westwards along the Trent & Mersey to Stoke on Trent, where the

*Escape to the hills –
with friends David
and Dorthe*

*Cycling with Stella
and her niece (Luci)
and nephew (Glenn)*

*Rupert Bear – our mascot
gets an outing too*

Potteries lined the canal bank in forlorn abandonment, then turning right onto the Caldon Canal, recently restored and offering a route back into the Staffordshire moors. It was a revelation. After battling through the choking weeds and rushes on the lower stretch above Etruria Junction, this lovely narrow canal winds and climbs up through the prettiest rural moorland, with villages and pubs to match. Then on to the more famous Macclesfield Canal and the Peak Forest Canal, wintering in the terminal basin at Whaley Bridge, back in Derbyshire. The following year we headed back to the Trent & Mersey, then eastwards to Chester on the Shropshire Union, and westwards on the celebrated Llangollen Canal, crossing the spectacular Pontcysllte Aquaduct. We returned via the Shropshire Union canal to Birmingham and Stafford, then back to Shardlow (near Derby). (see Inset *Memories of Morgan*)

Given *Morgan's* small size and fragility – especially when jostling with big steel narrow boats – this was quite a remarkable passage, involving long car journeys, careful winterisation plans to prevent damage from ice, and laborious fitting out in the Spring, a ritual that included squeezing Seelastic compound into the widening 'laps' between the clinker hull planks, applying coats of toxic anti-fouling to the bottom of the hull, and sprucing up the cabin as much as possible. The passage did not take place without incidents: a tramp sleeping on board at a boatyard in Marple, and leaving his mark in no uncertain fashion; a runaway horse pulling a trip barge from behind our mooring near Chester, the steerer frantically working his tiller to avoid the boat crashing into us; and numerous foulings of the propeller by weeds, plastic bags and general detritus, requiring a long lean over the stern with cutting gear. But he survived remarkably well, and after the second year of his travels he was back home in Derbyshire on the Trent & Mersey.

★ ★ ★

But *Morgan* wasn't our only recreational diversion. There were holidays abroad. France was the favourite, driving in Stella's Renault 5 down to Burgundy, Provence, and just about every other region in the country at one time or other. We over-nighted in charming old family hotels with delicious food on fixed menus, albeit with dingy rooms and dodgy plumbing, at ridiculously low prices. Sometimes boats were involved: a cabin cruiser on the delightful Charente in south west France, through Cognac for the brandy ; on the Nivernais in Burgundy; and on my MK mates Len and Co's restored Dutch Barge *Eagle River* on the Canal du Midi.

Group holidays featured as well: with Pete and Carolyn to Amsterdam and Brittany; with Tim and Carol to Provence, and later Portugal, taking the car by boat to Bilbao and Vigo, then driving southwards to Porto. And a big group holiday to the Greek islands of Skiathos, Skopelos, and Alonnissos, where a faux political argument developed about how the holiday should be organised, between the 'centralisers' led by Tim and Carol, and the quasi-anarchic 'devolvers', led by me, the 'bureaucratic guerrilla' and advocate of participatory democracy. It was a kind of joke, but it was argued forcefully; and in its highly localised and trivial way it perhaps unwittingly reflected some important underlying issues that faced us all in the years ahead – both for individual behaviour and political behaviour, especially for the nations and regions of Europe.

Stella, still fearful of flying after the Mexico experience, had travelled with me to Greece by train and boat to Athens, then by train to the east coast for the ferry to the islands. We returned via Mykonos, where we picked up a remarkable Russian cruise boat, full of politburo officials and fellow travellers from East Germany and Poland, who were not surprisingly perhaps very unforthcoming in response to our chat over the dinner table. There were also some West Germans, who stood aloof and smug, exposing their contempt for their East European cousins with an attitude bordering on crass vulgarity. We made friends with a couple of young French women returning from Vietnam, relishing our more neutral observer status.

Later we returned by car to Greece via Venice or Ancona, then by ferry to Patras, and on to Ithaca – reading Odysseus every morning by the 'wine-dark sea' before eating 'Fishes A or B' in the local taverna. Another year it was Corfu, watching the swallows maraud the old town, and cricket on the green. Later to Kefalonia, taking a small motor boat to jostle with the ferries in the harbour, and Paxos, an archetypically pretty waterside taverna in itself and on Jeremy Jefferies' recommendation, the tiny unspoilt island of Meganissi; further south, Crete, with its archaeology, seaside harbours, and Sumerian gorge to walk all day long.

★ ★ ★

Escape to Greece -Ithaca was the favourite

We were lucky to have the money and the time to enjoy these wonderful holidays abroad. By 1974 the long post war economic boom had come to an end. Inflation, rising raw material prices and confrontation with the miners forced Ted Heath to declare a three-day working week. He was forced to take the miners on and ask the public "Who Rules Britain? ". The public decided that it wasn't him (although the Conservatives won more votes, if less seats) and much to our delight after the shock Tory victory of 1970, Labour crept in, but with no overall majority. Harold Wilson returned as PM and Labour paid off the miners with a 35 per cent pay increase. But inflation and the trade deficit continued to rise, the government was forced to cut back on its spending plans and unemployment rose to levels not seen since the 1930s. By 1975 the Chancellor of the Exchequer Denis

Healey was introducing compulsory wage controls and going to the IMF for a loan of over £1 billion. Britain was becoming the 'sick man of Europe'.

Worse, the IRA was increasing its 'blitz on Britain' with bombings on the M62 (a coach carrying servicemen and their wives) Westminster Hall, and the Tower of London. Guildford and Birmingham followed with major loss of life. The Prevention of Terrorism Act that followed led in turn to a series of miscarriages of justice, as the police response appeared to be to arrest anyone they thought they could pin the bombings on and make sure the charges stuck by fair means or foul.

But up in Derbyshire we seemed to be immune from all this. We had secure jobs, a lovely environment away from urban unrest, and plenty of free time. Even our jobs, although intellectually and corporately challenging, were not overly stressful. We lived in a kind of north midlands pastoral refuge.

And creatively the country seemed to be booming. *Monty Python's Flying Circus* had attracted a huge following on TV, and went on to make several sensational films, including the controversial *Life Of Brian*. David Bowie, Queen and Pink Floyd were in full flow. The Who's *Tommy* was brilliantly filmed by Ken Russell.

But sadly, Alf Ramsey, architect of the 1966 World Cup win, and the team we saw play so well in Guadalajara in 1970 was sacked, having failed to steer England to the 1974 finals.

★ ★ ★

I am sitting on our small William Morris pattern covered sofa in our tiny 'sitting room' at Hazelnut Cottage, with the TV switched on. Brown Hessian covers the walls to hide the rising damp behind the sofa. The low beam across the ceiling is painted black. Stella is sitting beside me. We are watching the 1976 FA Cup Final between Manchester United – the team she supported as a girl – and 'my' Saints, Southampton, from the Second Division. We had been offered a ticket just the previous day by Tim in London, but had decided that neither of us could take it – it would be unfair. We would watch it on the box.

We are tense, excited. The game is tight, no clear breakthroughs. Southampton, well stocked with experienced players like Osgood, McCalliog and Channon, are holding their own, looking well controlled. Manchester, a young side, are not tearing them to pieces. This is not the Manchester of Law, Charlton and Best. But anything could happen.

And halfway through the second half it does. Channon passes to McCalliog and the old pro strokes a gorgeous defence splitting pass down the 'inside channel' where little Bobby Stokes, the junior in the side, latches on to it and steers it past the advancing Stepney into the corner of the net. I nearly hit the black beam in the ceiling over my head with a shout and a leap from the sofa. One of those magic footballing moments, matching that famous victory by the Cherries over Spurs back in 1957. Manchester fail to equalise. The Saints follow Sunderland as the only Second Division winners of the FA Cup.

The old sweats remember their drills

DAVID LACEY sees one of the big upsets in FA Cup history . . .

United fail to give best on the day

Manchester United 0 Southampton 1

Stella looks glum. I don't want to gloat, and slip out to the garden to tend joyously to the weeds, gazing down the sunny tree-blown valley.

★ ★ ★

By now my footballing interest had transferred from Bonsall Youth to the Derbyshire planners. We had a pretty good core of players in the Department and we put up a fair show in the local NALGO[6] league, losing out 1-0 to the Surveyors in a tense final of the tournament. I played in a central striking role and/or on the wing, delivering crosses 'Terry Paine' style[7] to be headed in

6   National Association of Local Government Officers
7   Terry Pain was the Saint's star right-winger in the 50s and 60s, and played for England in one of the World Cup matches of 1966

by one of our lively front men. Later one of the leading lights in the team recruited some of us to play for a local team in the Derby & District League. This was proper non-league football, and very competitive. Yet we held our own pretty well most of the time. But the deadly seriousness in which this football was taken – especially by the manager/coach – did not appeal to me. Football, like fishing, was to be enjoyed, not subjugated to a 'win at all cost' mentality. I clearly belonged to a previous era, infused with a Corinthian spirit: 'the game's the thing'.

Meanwhile the Saints had gained promotion to the First Division. I watched them wherever I could, in Manchester and Nottingham for example. They usually lost. But it was good to follow the team from where I was born.

★ ★ ★

I set out in *Morgan* on another journey, this time without Stella – she had 'retired ' from boating – south westwards along the Trent & Mersey and the Staffs & Worcester to the rivers Severn and Avon. Stourport was an early stopping place, moored in the Basin and drinking Ansell's Ales on the rambling lawns of the Tontine Hotel. But at Worcester the wash from passing trip boats gave *Morgan's* bottom a bashing, when he was moored temporarily along the quay in shallow water, and I had to run him for urgent repairs downriver to Tewkesbury and on to the Warwickshire Avon. Pershore was another fine stopping place, at a traditional boatyard near the weir. But more problems ensued: a neighbouring boat to which Morgan was roped leant over as the water level dropped in a period of very dry weather, pulling him below the water level. Fortunately the boatyard took responsibility and cleaned up the hull and engine – although they had to straighten out the piston rod in the process (it had got bent through attempting to start it with the crankcase full of water). Later the propeller shaft snapped cleanly and vertically in two, prompting another repair. *Morgan* was going through the wars. But eventually I reached Stratford-on-Avon, where I met up with an old friend and enjoyed the luxury of staying in a hotel; then on to Birmingham, experiencing the historic calm of the canal beneath the modern roar of Spaghetti Junction way overhead, before heading back to the Trent & Mersey and home, two years after I had begun.

I had become increasingly absorbed – even obsessed – by *Morgan's* travels. It wasn't just the interest and enjoyment of seeing England in a very different and fascinating way. It was also the challenge of keeping this little wooden clinker boat going, against all the odds.

★ ★ ★

Perhaps my enthusiasm for travelling England's canals and rivers was also prompted – consciously or unconsciously – by growing disillusion at work. The structure plan was grinding onwards in a complex process that was geared to technical forecasts of population and household growth, predicated on increasingly political assumptions about migration: "We're not having that level of in-migration from Nottingham!" said our boss in response to the trend forecasts identified by Dave. And this process was being undertaken through a steep vertical hierarchy comprising committee councillors, chief planner, assistant chief planner, group leader, team leaders, and senior planners. I was a long way from the delegated responsibility that I had in Newfoundland.

But in any case my real interest was moving away from this conventional 'top-down' approach to planning, and towards engaging the wider community in a more 'bottom-up' approach. In 1971 the Skeffington Report had set out a direction of travel that encouraged greater public participation, and there was considerable interest in the profession and in academia in developing genuine community engagement. But in practice it was undertaken more as a 'box-ticking' exercise based on consulting the public at specified stages of the plan-making process, on terms defined by the plan-makers rather than those being planned. And so it was with the Derbyshire Structure Plan: we consulted local people at evening meetings on 'strategic options' in areas defined by the technical process. Not surprisingly attendance was low – at one meeting just seven souls turned up. At another a group of four staged a walk-out because they argued they were assigned to the wrong area – local identity obviously overshadowing any technical definitions. These low responses in turn fed professional cynicism in the local planning authority: public participation was characterised by general apathy and specific interest from the 'usual suspects'. This attitude failed to recognise that this kind of 'public participation' was a sham, unable to engage the public on its own terms.

I met with fellow enthusiasts working on an innovative public participation exercise in Sheffield, and researchers at INLOGOV, a local government think-tank. I argued my case in Derbyshire, but received little support for any radical change in the face of the structure plan juggernaut. I was in good company. A major study of the many participation initiatives in the 1960s and 1970s concluded that:

> *Though there have been great moves towards public involvement in recent years, little has been achieved by way of a fundamental shift in power, a shift which implicitly underlay the ideas of radical proponents of participation in the late 1960s. In the end, elite perspectives have won out, and participation has served the purposes of building up a consensus for the proposals of those in power, thereby legitimising them.* [8]

My involvement in active participation extended beyond my professional duties in structure planning. I signed on as a WEA[9] tutor, helping people to understand the planning system and influence it. This was an informal method of 'planning aid', first developed by the Town and Country Planning Institute (TCPA) and later by the Royal Town Planning Institute(RTPI). In Matlock I worked with Chris Charlton, a key mover and shaker in the prestigious Arkwright Society and an archetypal 'usual suspect' who kept a close eye on the policies

---

8   Boaden et al(1982): Public Participation in Local Services (London: Longman)

9   Workers Educational Institute

and decisions of local bodies, especially with regard to conservation and heritage matters. Most of the issues I got involved in were concerned with village planning and design. But in Derby I got involved in heavier matters. Fiona, an enthusiastic local WEA tutor, set up a course on planning in a neighbourhood of terraced streets in Derby, distributing leaflets to advertise it. Nearly one hundred citizens, mostly of Asian descent, showed up. I was there to explain the procedures and possibilities of the English planning system. They were there to find out if their homes were going to be pulled down. We had made the fundamental mistake underlying many participation exercises: not being crystal clear (and honest) about what the exercise was intended to achieve.

Chris Charlton and I worked on another planning matter closer to home: the proposed extension of a major quarry near Bonsall, off Clatterway. This raised fears of danger to nearby houses through blasting, and increased lorry traffic. There were arguments about whether the quarry was really about mining high quality lead, or low quality felspar, and how much employment it would generate. Expert geologists were brought in. A local action group was set up. To its credit, Derbyshire Planning Department allowed those of us not directly involved with the proposal in the department to act on behalf of the action group. Months of research and discussion ensued, with Chris a key advisor. Derbyshire's planning department played it cool, acting almost as a 'neutral' convenor for both sides of the argument, although of course in the end it would be responsible for making the decision. That decision was essentially a political one. Jobs and the economy were paramount, and in the end they over-rode the environmental impact and risk of danger to homes, despite the mixed evidence surrounding these issues. The application was approved. To his credit, Cllr Bookbinder, leader of the council, explained the decision with honesty, recognising the villagers' case. Due process had been undertaken, even if many of us thought the substantive decision was faulty. I wrote up the story as a case study.[10]

Both Stella and I were also involved in a local Shelter group campaigning for better policies and decisions to alleviate homelessness and poor housing conditions. Although very small – a handful of people led by a Liberal activist with experience in Liverpool – we had some success at publicising local problems and effecting modest change. Shelter's reputation as a well known charity clearly helped.

* * *

By now I was looking for change. Mainstream planning was reaching a dead end for me. The structure plan suddenly sprouted as politicians demanded clear directions, and the complex technical processes we had been working on in several teams was suddenly reduced to simplistic solutions on the back of the proverbial fag-packet. My creative ideas about 'beads on a string' to allocate housing at stations on the rail line between Derby and Matlock, in order to maximise

10   *Ball Eye Quarry: a case study in local planning conflict*

public transport and reduce the kind of car travel generated by sprawling estates on the edge of towns, had long been subsumed by the realities of speculative land development. I had lost interest. And from a purely personal perspective about my future I had looked around me in the office, especially 'upwards' and thought: this is not for me.

My search for a different future took some bizarre turns. I was interested in other lifestyles, such as 'dropping out' altogether by joining a commune to write, grow vegetables and just 'be'. I even visited one in the South East to explore the possibilities. I was approached by 'headhunters' seeking professional planners to work in Libya on new communities : they were scouring the world for professional experts and looked to Britain – renowned for its new towns – for planners. I was interviewed in Manchester and London and offered a job. When I explained that my wife was a planner too, they offered her a job as well. I researched Libya and found out another story from the usual mad dictator stuff: much higher levels of literacy, health and employment than the West. Gadafi had clearly directed much of his oil wealth for the benefit of the general population. I was keen to go – like Newfoundland, for the adventure, come what may. But Stella was not convinced, nor could she really believe it to be 'real'. This time I remained in England.

So instead I began to think seriously about a more realistic option – teaching and research.

★ ★ ★

I arrive home one evening, unlock the front door, and open the door to the sitting room – I want to catch the news. But the sitting room is full of women – so many I can't tell how many or who. I retreat in confusion, to friendly laughter all round. I am literally taken aback.

I had forgotten that Stella was hosting her women's group. This had been going for some time in the Matlock area. The Women's Lib movement had taken off at the beginning of the decade with the publication of Germaine Greer's *Female Eunuch* and had gone from strength to strength. In the political chaos and confusion of the 70s it was perhaps the one social and political campaign that had grown and flourished. For Stella it was really important, and I supported her feminism. What I wasn't clear about was how it impacted on our relationship, or what my role – if any – was in this new movement.

Stella had also grown tired of her work in Monitoring & Intelligence, working away in the labyrinth of Derbyshire's bureaucratic hierarchies. As before, she wanted to make a more direct impact. She switched careers to librarianship, taking a big salary drop to work for the County Library. Later she took a Masters Degree in Information Science at the University of Sheffield, which meant commuting across the Peak District, often in atrocious winter conditions. But she enjoyed it and did well, earning a well deserved Distinction.

But in more ways than one we were slowly drifting apart.

★ ★ ★

120

Labour was still in power, and Callaghan had replaced Wilson as PM. But the economy was still struggling and the government was trying to keep the lid on pay. The Unions were rebelling, and Tony Benn was leading the left of the Party with popular support in the ranks. But he was narrowly defeated in an election for Deputy Leader against Dennis Healey. The winter of discontent followed later. Whether Benn winning would have changed the course of British politics will remain a matter of speculation.

I had joined the local Labour Party, meeting in upstairs rooms of various pubs. The West Derbyshire constituency was rock solid Conservative, but our membership was good with a lively bunch of leaders and activists. Here I met Annie, a local teacher. Intelligent, vivacious, with striking blonde hair, she loved literature and music, and was great company. As one who had grown up on a council estate she also had a strong sense of social justice.

Meanwhile I was still looking for a new direction in my work. I applied for lecturing jobs. At Oxford Polytechnic I don't think my spotted yellow tie impressed, nor my emphasis on research and learning rather than actually teaching students. At Sheffield University I apparently did quite well but 'faded' at the end. At Nottingham University the interview did not go well: clearly my non-professional reading did not pass muster, and there was a knowing arrogance between the interviewers which irritated me. Finally, I did shine quite well at Leicester Polytechnic and to my surprise I was offered a post as Senior Lecturer in the School of Building and Estate Management. I decided to take it.

Farewell Card from Derbyshire

My planning days with Derbyshire were over. But they gave me a good send-off.

★ ★ ★

Meanwhile *Morgan* was in decline. I took him to Trevithick's boatyard in Nottingham, on the canal that linked the Trent & Mersey to the River Trent near Trent Bridge. This was one of the few yards making and repairing wooden boats – Tom Trevithick had worked on building and repairing the old Trent barges. He lived on site but was getting on, and his eyesight was failing. He had 'apprenticed' a younger man to take over the work – and maybe one day the Yard. When I tied *Morgan* up in the Yard's private dry dock I knew he was in good hands.

But I also planned to get a bigger boat. I bought a fine ex-naval pinnace constructed of double-diagonal planked mahogany. *Troutbridge* had a central cockpit, two two-berth cabins forward and aft, and a galley and Loo. The man who sold it to me spent a long time telling me what he had done and showing off its qualities. It was indeed a fine boat and capable of taking a bigger crew. Stella and friends Pete and Carolyn, and Tim and Carol, came on its first major outing.

We set off from its moorings at Long Eaton down to the bottom lock, out into the Trent. It is a hot sunny day.

"Can you fend off at the front?" I shout to several of my crew, lounging on the front deck, as we approach the lock. No response. I am having trouble finding reverse gear on the crash gear box. I shout again. Somebody looks up, as if woken by some strange sound. By now the lock is looming. What is it about boats that makes people go into instant lounge mode? Maybe it is the warmth of the sun, and the quiet of the canal. Whatever it is, the silence soon ends. With a bang and a crunch we hit the lock apron. I swear very loudly. The Navy Lark Part One.

Fortunately the double diagonal planks hold well, and survive with a scrape. We lock through to the Trent, and cruise upriver.

"Eeeuuuugh!!!". From below. The Loo. Poor Carol. The traditional pump-handled toilet has back-fired, geysering shit, paper and water up and onto her in the little cubicle. It is horrible, and Carol is distraught. All hands below deck. Pete confesses that he has used a lot of paper, which has probably caused the blockage. We clear up Carol and the boat as best we can. Navy Lark Part Two.

Later I take some friends from work on a more

Troutbridge with crew on the river Trent

successful trip down the Trent to Newark, but I never get the hang of the gearbox. Meanwhile Trevithick's have done a terrific job on Morgan, its clinker hull fully repaired and shining white. Within the year I sell *Troutbridge* and take up again with *Morgan*.

★ ★ ★

By 1978 I was now commuting from Bonsall to Leicester. This meant a short drive down to the pretty little station at Cromford to catch the local Matlock train to Derby, there changing for Leicester. I had left the cosy social cocoon of County Hall in Matlock for the wider, colder world. And with the rail strikes and disruptions of the winter of discontent I spent a lot of time on a very draughty Leicester Station.

Leicester Poly seemed large and anonymous after Derbyshire. I knew no-one apart from my immediate colleagues. Norma, my new boss as head of the planning group, asked me to give my first lecture on the subject of mining and land reclamation, assuming that as I had worked in Derbyshire I would be familiar with this subject. In fact I knew next to nothing about it. So I spent hours in the Library researching and cobbling together a presentation. I also knew next to nothing about lecturing. If I was to give say five lectures a week, how many hours would I have to spend in the Library ?

I gaze down from my lecturn to a lecture theatre seating forty or fifty students of construction and surveying. Many of them are Asian. My imaginary 'model' of a lecture is some kind of grand peroration in an Oxbridge college or the Royal Society, full of carefully rehearsed descriptions, analysis and conclusions. I read my quasi essay verbatim. The students try to write down every word. But I am talking too fast for them to do this properly. Some of them give up and look around nervously. Others scribble furiously, occasionally leaning over to copy something from the student sitting next to them. None of them, I am pretty sure, are understanding a word of anything I am saying. Welcome to the world of Higher Education.

It gets better. With Norma I work on course development, planning new courses in planning and development for Hons approval by CNAA, the national regulatory body. I enjoy this, and we work well together. And I get to run the mainstream planning module. With another colleague, Lutz Luithlen, a charismatic and imaginative architect of Prussian descent, I work on some rural planning modules which include an annual field trip with some general studies students. We spend inordinate amounts of time planning these trips with another tutor from the Geography Department, Clive Harrison – to Durham, Bristol, Derbyshire and Southampton. The staff-student ratio works out at about 2 or 3 to one on this module, undetected because we are in different administrative sections of the Polytechnic… And the quality of this teaching is high, carefully planned with background reading and meetings with local professionals. It is fascinating fun – for the tutors anyway.

I enjoy the work but the commuting is tedious. Sometimes I stay over with Norma at her house in the comfortable suburbs of Leicester. She has recently divorced and lives alone with her two children. She is an excellent host, a great cook, attractive and warm company. I am outside my comfortable Derbyshire cocoon and feel estranged. I fail to prevent the inevitable.

★ ★ ★

I am chugging fast across the floor of a small, dark crowded bar in Brussels, dancing to Little Eva's *Locomotion*, (one of my favourite rock-pop songs, written by the great Carole King and Gerry Coffin) in a state of fairly advanced inebriation. This is much to the amusement of my fellow tutors and students on a weekend 'study tour' of the European capital. All I see is laughing faces around me, dark shapes huddled against the bar, and in the light behind the bar a *patron* who does *not* look amused. My chugging gets more frenetic. I am in dance heaven.

I am dimly aware of movement round the bar. Suddenly one of my colleagues, Bill Maxted, is trying to get my attention.

"Trev, we've got to get out of here, the Barman says we must go."

"Wass the problem ?" I shout.

"There's some guys with guns, they don't like the look of us. We've got to get out."

I stagger to the door. Bill helps me out. Some students support me as we stagger back to our hotel. Somebody says something about Belgian Nazis. The party is over.

On the following Monday I walk into the lecture theatre for my regular lecture on planning methodology. There is giggling laughter and a cheer goes up. They have discovered that I am a normal human being, and I am accepted. I realise that it was an inadvertently cheap way to play to the gallery, and against approved pedagogical principles. But it did make teaching easier.

★ ★ ★

Bill was a good mate at Leicester, and he put me up some nights in his rented cottage out in the Leicestershire countryside. He came from Southampton and was a fellow Saints supporter. He was good company and we shared our views of work and the Department. One evening we travelled down to London for the evening to see the Saints lose to Arsenal, and one summer we met up to walk some of the Dorset Coast.

Bill was a welcome relief from the typical intrigues of academic life. Not that I didn't make my own contributions to office gossip. I loved Norma and we had a good working relationship, but I couldn't see our relationship working in the longer run. I was also behaving as if off the leash, flirting with inappropriate enthusiasm with one of the technicians and even a couple of students – thankfully no more than flirting. But my 'moral compass' was swinging around a bit. Meanwhile back in Derbyshire, Stella was having an affair with one of *her* colleagues. And I started spending more weekend time with Annie – my girlfriend from the Labour Party – in the warm and lively bars of Matlock Bath. Annie was great, with the most beautiful face, and full of life and love. And I loved her to bits. But I was all over the place.

Leicester Poly was well run and there were good prospects. But I wanted to teach and research 'proper' planning, rather than planning for surveyors and estate agents. A Course Leader job came up in Cheltenham at the Gloucestershire College of Art and Technology, specialising in rural planning. Just my thing.

I was invited for interview, which went well. One of the other candidates was a very good design planner I had known from Milton Keynes days, so I knew the competition was stiff. I was quite surprised when a few days later I was offered the job.

From a professional point of view it was a mad move. The Thatcher government had shockingly won the 1979 election, and if it survived – after an early difficult period of recession and unemployment – the prospects for planning and higher education looked grim. Norma, and the new Head of Department Dave Chiddick (dubbed 'SuperChid' by Bill Maxted) advised against. "Careering around" was how he aptly described it.

But sitting by the path one sunny day above Hazelnut Cottage I knew I had to go. Stella and I were now far apart emotionally, living different lives, and with different relationships. I didn't want to leave her or Derbyshire, but I felt I had no choice. I gazed down at our cottage and the dry stone walls of the valley below. It was as beautiful as ever. So was Stella, and I still loved her. But I had to move on.

Chapter 5

Epilogue

The 1970s had begun with the flower-powering of the Sixties cultural revolution, an outpouring of exotic music, clothes and lifestyles. Photographs of families and friends reveal lengths of hair, flairs and skirts that seem from another world of pink, orange, and vermilion. We look back on the decade with a nostalgic giggle and some disbelief.

But the underlying economic and political tides were flowing out. The oil crisis of 1973 marked the beginning of the end of an era of growth symbolised by Harold Wilson's "white-hot revolution". Recurring economic crises generated a 'stagflation' that undermined the Labour Party's attempts to cure the "sick man of Europe", epitomised when Denis Healey had to go to the IMF for financial help in 1975. Tony Benn's narrow failure to win a Labour Party Deputy Leader election closed off a radical socialist avenue for change, whilst arguably the rejection of Barbara Castle's *In Place of Strife* also marked the end of the road for a rapprochement between industry and the unions under a Labour government, and paved the way for the Thatcherite revolution that followed.

But this is a view in hindsight. In Derbyshire we escaped much of this apparent decline. Both of us were earning good salaries with a low mortgage in a delightful environment. I was working in the mainstream of my career, with intelligent and very likeable colleagues. I was still playing football, sometimes even fishing in the delightful rivers of the Wye, Derwent and Dovedale. Our exploration of the waterways of England – and sometimes France – continued apace. Electing not to have children, we had the time and the money to travel abroad as well as hosting many friends and family who came to visit us in Bonsall. In many ways it was the best of times for us.

And while economic and political difficulties increased during the decade – the IRA bombing campaign added fuel to the fire – there were also other more positive changes. Environmental and ecological movements grew. We joined the Common Market. And perhaps most importantly of all, Women's Lib (as it was called then) flourished, achieving real gains in equality in the workplace and changing age-old stereotypes in the home. Stella was at the forefront of that movement, and I supported her as well as I could in the gender revolution.

How that revolution impacted on our personal relationship is a more complex story. I had been the would-be 'new man' in a would-be model couple of our generation. But whether relevant or not, our relationship had substantially broken down, to the extent that although we were still friends, I could not continue it. Like the 70's themselves, the bright flowering of our early marriage had declined into something more tarnished.

But I could not foresee the kind of turmoil that would follow in the next decade.

★ ★ ★

Starry starry night – Stella`s painting of Hazelnut Cottage